THE AJAX

OF

SOPHOCLES.

WITH

NOTES,

CRITICAL AND EXPLANATORY.

BY

C. E. PALMER, M.A.

LONDON:

GEORGE BELL AND SONS,

YORK STREET, COVENT GARDEN.

1878.

This scarce antiquarian book is included in our special *Legacy Reprint Series*. In the interest of creating a more extensive selection of rare historical book reprints, we have chosen to reproduce this title even though it may possibly have occasional imperfections such as missing and blurred pages, missing text, poor pictures, markings, dark backgrounds and other reproduction issues beyond our control. Because this work is culturally important, we have made it available as a part of our commitment to protecting, preserving and promoting the world's literature.

PREFACE.

ONE object which I have kept in view in the writing of these notes has been to adapt them to the requirements of the younger student. In some of them, where I have thought that the passage under discussion had not been satisfactorily explained by previous editors, and I have expounded it in a new way, the reasons assigned by me for such an exposition may seem rather to appeal to the judgment of the more advanced scholar. This also may be the case where former critics and editors have differed between themselves as to the meaning of a passage, and where out of two or more expositions of it, I have endeavoured to show which of them is the right one. The text is one of my own selection in each particular case, for I consider it to be the proper function of every editor of a Greek Play in the first place to form his own judgment on the question what may be the right reading, quite as much as it is for him in the second place to decide what may be in his opinion the proper sense of it. A critical examination is as necessary in the one case as in the other, insomuch that any editor seems to desert his post who implicitly adopts the text of some distinguished textuary, simply because it happens to be the one which is most commonly used in schools and universities. Such an editor lays himself open to the attack, that while he makes the best apology he can for perhaps a very poor conjectural emendation, and ignores its faults, he has yet passed by in silence a reading which perhaps has not only the testimony of all the MSS., but which, when fairly examined, may be in every respect perfectly unobjectionable, except in the supposed fault of metre. With respect to the metre of the lyrical parts, I have long entertained a suspicion, which in some cases has ripened into a conviction, that the poet allowed himself a freer licence than editors have assigned to him. The subject of lyrical metre has, I believe, been very imperfectly understood even by those who have professed themselves to be masters of the art, and have written treatises on it. In the preface to my notes on the Oedipus Coloneus published in 1860, I even then spoke of those emendations which were made merely for the sake of metre as follows: "In most of these cases no fault has been found with the sense of the passage, with the propriety of its expressions, or anything else except the metre. For this and other reasons it has appeared to me that the stringent laws laid down by metrical critics cannot in all cases be maintained, unless we suppose a much greater number of verses to have been negligently transcribed or designedly altered than is by any means probable. I am inclined to think that there was a certain margin of licence which dramatic writers allowed themselves not yet accurately defined by metrical theorists. Hence their laws are probably more stringent than those by which the poet was bound." What was then put forth as a probable opinion I have, I think, now proved to be a fact, as far as regards the deviations from a choriambus in corresponding lines in some of the plays of Sophocles. I have shown that the deviations are all comprised within certain very intelligible and definable limits which may well be defended on the ordinary principles of metre in other cases, and that if those limits had been transgressed, which they are not, we could not have defended them as a poetical licence on any known principles of metre. The line of argument which has been followed out by me to its inevitable conclusion, approaches almost by an evanescent quantity to absolute demonstration. Inasmuch as it bears on the foregoing remarks on the text and the metre of Sophocles, I here take occasion to insert the greater part of a letter from the late Professor Conington, which will be read with much more interest than anything which I could say further on those subjects.

"124, High Street, Oxford, Feb. 4, 1861.

"MY DEAR SIR,—I ought to have written sooner to thank you for your kind present of the Oedipus Coloneus, especially as my occupations will not allow me now to make more than a simple acknowledgment. The subject, however, is one which interests me very much, and in proof of it I may tell you that I had already bought your book when the presentation copy arrived. Though Aeschylus has been my chief study, I have at various times paid a good deal of attention to Sophocles, and I have long regretted that his text should have been so unscrupulously dealt with as it has been by recent editors. More than once I have thought of calling attention to the subject, and I have made an effort, which perhaps may one day succeed, to get Dindorf's text superseded in our University examinations. Dindorf, I suppose, is the chief offender—at all events he has more vogue in England than any of the others, and the edition which he has just printed at our University press (the engagement being one which was made with him ten years ago, in the lifetime of the late Dean Gaisford), though containing more commonly useful information than most of his works, is certainly no improvement on its predecessors, so far as the text goes. I am not sure that I do not think your language about emendatory criticism rather too sweeping, and the character which the quotation from the Quarterly assigns to the Germans, however applicable to individuals, is surely unjust to the whole nation. To make the interpretation and criticism of the classics a *national* question would, I think, be unfortunate in itself, and hardly likely to be successful in the present paucity of men in England who have the time, the inclination, or the ability to edit the classics. We ought rather to be glad to get any help from any source, while we may fairly hope that the progress of sound criticism will in time explode these novelties, as it has exploded many others. Cobet,[1] in the preface to his Observationes Criticae in Scriptores Graecos (a work, by-the-bye, which though rather of the innovating school is very valuable as showing what errors have been committed by transcribers of MSS.), says that many of Ahrens and Meineke's conjectures on Theocritus which are now praised will in time share the fate of Valcknaer's, which also were greatly praised in their day: and so you and I may console ourselves with thinking that Hermann and Dindorf's improvements of the dramatists will in many cases come to be thought as little of as Brunck and Schütz's now are. As to emendatory criticism, I scarcely think that much is gained by laying down general rules. The real question is about the state of the MSS. of the particular author, which in one case may be very good, and in another deplorably bad. To take the two authors of whom I know most; in Virgil I should always lean strongly against change, the MSS. being in general so good. In Aeschylus, though experience has made me more conservative than I was, I should think the antecedent probability for or against a correction much more evenly balanced. As to Sophocles I have no right to speak, never having given that study to his text which only a critical editor can give; but two things have impressed themselves on me from such imperfect study of him as I have been able to make. The first is what you dwell upon with regard to the metres. It seems to me, as I am glad to find it seems to you, that in many of the lyric parts the sense is exceedingly good where the metre is apparently inconformable. You, I see, suppose that in such cases Sophocles' notions of metre are freer than those for which the editors have given him credit. I had rather thought that they were cases in which the metrical conformity had been hopelessly obliterated by the Alexandrine

---

[1] I do not know whether I have read this word aright. It is a new name to me.

PREFACE. vii

critics, but as I am no metrist myself, I shall be very glad to be better taught. But my *conclusion* has been precisely the same as yours, that when the sense and language are right, an editor ought not to rewrite the passage, simply for the metre's sake. I speak of rewriting, not of slight alterations, which I do not object to, if they are easy and natural. . . . . . .
Excuse the haste with which I have been obliged to scribble off this letter, and believe me

"Yours very faithfully,
"JOHN CONINGTON."

Some of the following notes are the result of long and patient consideration of the passages to which they refer. I was dissatisfied with the interpretation usually given to them. It presented to my mind a difficulty which again and again would recur to me, until at length what I believe to be the right solution came suddenly into my mind. I could never, for instance, be satisfied with the manner in which the following passage in vv. 337, 338 was usually construed,—

ἀνὴρ ἔοικεν ἢ νοσεῖν, ἢ τοῖς πάλαι
νοσήμασι ξυνοῦσι λυπεῖσθαι παρών.

And certainly for more than two years I continued to be so perplexed with it, that I thought I should be obliged either to pass it over in silence, or to express my conviction that the common interpretation of it could not be the right one. At length a more careful consideration of the state of Ajax's mind as described by the Chorus in other parts of the Play, convinced me that the Chorus alluded to a mental malady that was still afflicting him, and had continued to do so from the moment of his recovering his consciousness. Although I am doubtful about the general character of my notes, and their suitability to the use and instruction of the younger student, I still hope that both learners and teachers will take a lively interest in any attempts of mine, wherein I may appear to have succeeded, in redeeming a passage from needless emendation, or in elucidating one which had been misinterpreted, or in bringing again to notice that which had been cast aside as worthless and hopelessly corrupt.

GREAT TORRINGTON,
 Nov. 3, 1877.

ΣΟΦΟΚΛΕΟΥΣ ΑΙΑΣ.

TA TOY ΔΡΑΜΑΤΟΣ ΠΡΟΣΩΠΑ.

ΑΘΗΝΑ.
ΟΔΥΣΣΕΥΣ.
ΑΙΑΣ.
ΧΟΡΟΣ ΣΑΛΑΜΙΝΙΩΝ ΝΑΥΤΩΝ.
ΤΕΚΜΗΣΣΑ.
ΑΓΓΕΛΟΣ.
ΤΕΥΚΡΟΣ.
ΜΕΝΕΛΑΟΣ.
ΑΓΑΜΕΜΝΩΝ.
ΕΥΡΥΣΑΚΗΣ ⎫
ΠΑΙΔΑΓΩΓΟΣ ⎬ κωφὰ πρόσωπα.
ΣΤΡΑΤΟΚΗΡΥΞ ⎭

ΥΠΟΘΕΣΙΣ.

Τὸ δρᾶμα τῆς Τρωϊκῆς ἐστι πραγματείας, ὥσπερ οἱ ΑΝΤΗΝΟΡΙΔΑΙ, καὶ ΑΙΧΜΑΛΩΤΙΔΕΣ, καὶ ΕΛΕΝΗΣ ΑΡΠΑΓΗ, καὶ ΜΕΜΝΩΝ. πεπτωκότος γὰρ ἐν τῇ μάχῃ τοῦ Ἀχιλλέως ἐδόκουν Αἴας τε καὶ Ὀδυσσεὺς ἐπ' αὐτῷ πλέον τι ἀριστεύειν περὶ τὴν τοῦ σώματος κομιδήν· καὶ κρινομένων περὶ τῶν ὅπλων κρατεῖ Ὀδυσσεύς. ὅθεν ὁ Αἴας, τῆς κρίσεως μὴ τυχὼν, παρακεκίνηται καὶ διέφθαρται τὴν γνώμην, ὥστε ἐφαπτόμενος τῶν ποιμνίων δοκεῖν τοὺς Ἕλληνας διαχρήσασθαι. καὶ τὰ μὲν ἀνεῖλε τῶν τετραπόδων, τὰ δὲ δήσας ἀπάγει ἐπὶ τὴν σκηνήν· ἐν οἷς ἐστι καὶ κριός τις ἔξοχος, ὃν ᾤετο εἶναι Ὀδυσσέα, ὃν δήσας ἐμαστίγωσεν, ὅθεν καὶ τῇ ἐπιγραφῇ πρόσκειται ὁ ΜΑΣΤΙΓΟΦΟΡΟΣ, ἢ πρὸς ἀντιδιαστολὴν τοῦ ΛΟΚΡΟΥ. Δικαίαρχος δὲ ΑΙΑΝΤΟΣ ΘΑΝΑΤΟΝ ἐπιγράφει. ἐν δὲ ταῖς διδασκαλίαις ψιλῶς ΑΙΑΣ ἀναγέγραπται.

Ταῦτα μὲν οὖν πράττει ὁ Αἴας· καταλαμβάνει δὲ Ἀθηνᾶ Ὀδυσσέα ἐπὶ τῆς σκηνῆς διοπτεύοντα τί ποτε ἄρα πράττει ὁ Αἴας, καὶ δηλοῖ αὐτῷ τὰ πραχθέντα, καὶ προκαλεῖται εἰς τὸ ἐμφανὲς τὸν Αἴαντα ἔτι ἐμμανῆ ὄντα, καὶ ἐπικομπάζοντα, ὡς τῶν ἐχθρῶν ἀνῃρημένων. καὶ ὁ μὲν εἰσέρχεται ὡς ἐπὶ τῷ μαστιγοῦν τὸν Ὀδυσσέα. παραγίνεται δὲ χορὸς Σαλαμινίων ναυτῶν, εἰδὼς μὲν τὸ γεγονὸς, ὅτι ποίμνια ἐσφάγησαν Ἑλληνικὰ, ἀγνοῶν δὲ τὸν δράσαντα. ἔξεισι δὲ καὶ Τέκμησσα, τοῦ Αἴαντος αἰχμάλωτος παλλακὶς, εἰδυῖα μὲν τὸν σφαγέα τῶν ποιμνίων ὅτι Αἴας ἐστὶν, ἀγνοοῦσα δὲ τίνος εἶεν τὰ ποίμνια. ἑκάτερος οὖν παρ' ἑκατέρου μαθόντες τὸ ἀγνοούμενον, ὁ χορὸς μὲν παρὰ Τεκμήσσης, ὅτι ὁ Αἴας ταῦτα ἔδρασε, Τέκμησσα δὲ παρὰ τοῦ χοροῦ, ὅτι Ἑλληνικὰ τὰ σφαγέντα ποίμνια, ἀπολοφύρονται· καὶ μάλιστα ὁ χορός. ὅθεν δὴ ὁ Αἴας προελθὼν ἔμφρων γενόμενος ἑαυτὸν ἀπολοφύρεται. καὶ τούτου ἡ Τέκμησσα δεῖται παύσασθαι τῆς ὀργῆς· ὁ δὲ ὑποκρινόμενος πεπαῦσθαι ἔξεισι καθαρ-

ΥΠΟΘΕΣΙΣ.

Τὸ δρᾶμα τῆς Τρωϊκῆς ἐστι πραγματείας, ὥσπερ οἱ ΑΝΤΗ-ΝΟΡΙΔΑΙ, καὶ ΑΙΧΜΑΛΩΤΙΔΕΣ, καὶ ΕΛΕΝΗΣ ΑΡΠΑΓΗ, καὶ ΜΕΜΝΩΝ. πεπτωκότος γὰρ ἐν τῇ μάχῃ τοῦ Ἀχιλλέως ἐδόκουν Αἴας τε καὶ Ὀδυσσεὺς ἐπ' αὐτῷ πλέον τι ἀριστεύειν περὶ τὴν τοῦ σώματος κομιδήν· καὶ κρινομένων περὶ τῶν ὅπλων κρατεῖ Ὀδυσσεύς. ὅθεν ὁ Αἴας, τῆς κρίσεως μὴ τυχὼν, παρακεκίνηται καὶ διέφθαρται τὴν γνώμην, ὥστε ἐφαπτόμενος τῶν ποιμνίων δοκεῖν τοὺς Ἕλληνας διαχρήσασθαι. καὶ τὰ μὲν ἀνεῖλε τῶν τετραπόδων, τὰ δὲ δήσας ἀπάγει ἐπὶ τὴν σκηνήν· ἐν οἷς ἐστι καὶ κριός τις ἔξοχος, ὃν ᾤετο εἶναι Ὀδυσσέα, ὃν δήσας ἐμαστίγωσεν, ὅθεν καὶ τῇ ἐπιγραφῇ πρόσκειται ὁ ΜΑΣΤΙΓΟΦΟΡΟΣ, ἢ πρὸς ἀντιδιαστολὴν τοῦ ΛΟΚΡΟΥ. Δικαίαρχος δὲ ΑΙΑΝΤΟΣ ΘΑΝΑΤΟΝ ἐπιγράφει. ἐν δὲ ταῖς διδασκαλίαις ψιλῶς ΑΙΑΣ ἀναγέγραπται.

Ταῦτα μὲν οὖν πράττει ὁ Αἴας· καταλαμβάνει δὲ Ἀθηνᾶ Ὀδυσσέα ἐπὶ τῆς σκηνῆς διοπτεύοντα τί ποτε ἄρα πράττει ὁ Αἴας, καὶ δηλοῖ αὐτῷ τὰ πραχθέντα, καὶ προκαλεῖται εἰς τὸ ἐμφανὲς τὸν Αἴαντα ἔτι ἐμμανῆ ὄντα, καὶ ἐπικομπάζοντα, ὡς τῶν ἐχθρῶν ἀνῃρημένων. καὶ ὁ μὲν εἰσέρχεται ὡς ἐπὶ τῷ μαστιγοῦν τὸν Ὀδυσσέα. παραγίνεται δὲ χορὸς Σαλαμινίων ναυτῶν, εἰδὼς μὲν τὸ γεγονός, ὅτι ποίμνια ἐσφάγησαν Ἑλληνικά, ἀγνοῶν δὲ τὸν δράσαντα. ἔξεισι δὲ καὶ Τέκμησσα, τοῦ Αἴαντος αἰχμάλωτος παλλακίς, εἰδυῖα μὲν τὸν σφαγέα τῶν ποιμνίων ὅτι Αἴας ἐστίν, ἀγνοοῦσα δὲ τίνος εἶεν τὰ ποίμνια. ἑκάτερος οὖν παρ' ἑκατέρου μαθόντες τὸ ἀγνοούμενον, ὁ χορὸς μὲν παρὰ Τεκμήσσης, ὅτι ὁ Αἴας ταῦτα ἔδρασε, Τέκμησσα δὲ παρὰ τοῦ χοροῦ, ὅτι Ἑλληνικὰ τὰ σφαγέντα ποίμνια, ἀπολοφύρονται· καὶ μάλιστα ὁ χορός. ὅθεν δὴ ὁ Αἴας προελθὼν ἔμφρων γενόμενος ἑαυτὸν ἀπολοφύρεται. καὶ τούτου ἡ Τέκμησσα δεῖται παύσασθαι τῆς ὀργῆς· ὁ δὲ ὑποκρινόμενος πεπαῦσθαι ἔξεισι καθαρσίων ἕνεκα καὶ ἑαυτὸν διαχρῆται. εἰσὶ δὲ καὶ ἐπὶ τῷ τέλει τοῦ δράματος λόγοι τινὲς Τεύκρου πρὸς Μενέλαον, οὐκ ἐῶντα θάπτειν τὸ σῶμα. τὸ δὲ πέρας, θάψας αὐτὸν Τεῦκρος ἀπολοφύρεται. παρίστησι δὲ ὁ λόγος τῆς τραγῳδίας ὅτι ἐξ ὀργῆς καὶ φιλονεικίας οἱ ἄνθρωποι ἥκοιεν ἐπὶ τὰ τοιαῦτα νοσήματα, ὥσπερ ὁ Αἴας προσδοκήσας ἐγκρατὴς εἶναι τῶν ὅπλων, καὶ ἀποτυχὼν ἔγνω ἑαυτὸν ἀνελεῖν. αἱ δὲ τοιαῦται φιλονεικίαι οὐκ εἰσὶν ἐπωφελεῖς οὐδὲ τοῖς δοκοῦσι νενικηκέναι. ὅρα γὰρ καὶ παρ' Ὁμήρῳ τὰ περὶ τῆς ἥττης τοῦ Αἴαντος πάνυ διὰ βραχέων καὶ περιπαθῶς· (Ὀδ. λ. 542.)

οἴη δ' Αἴαντος ψυχὴ Τελαμωνιάδαο
νόσφιν ἀφειστήκει κεχολωμένη εἵνεκα τευχέων.

εἶτα αὐτοῦ ἄκουε τοῦ κεκρατηκότος· (547.)

ὡς δὴ μὴ ὄφελον νικᾶν τοιῷδ' ἐπ' ἀέθλῳ.

οὐκ ἐλυσιτέλησεν ἄρα αὐτῷ ἡ νίκη, τοιούτου ἀνδρὸς διὰ τὴν ἧτταν ἀποθανόντος.

Ἡ σκηνὴ τοῦ δράματος ἐν τῷ ναυστάθμῳ πρὸς τῇ σκηνῇ τοῦ Αἴαντος. δαιμονίως δὲ εἰσφέρει προλογίζουσαν τὴν Ἀθηνᾶν. ἀπίθανον γὰρ τὸν Αἴαντα προϊόντα εἰπεῖν περὶ τῶν αὑτῷ πεπραγμένων, ὥσπερ ἐξελέγχοντα ἑαυτόν· οὐδὲ μὴν ἕτερός τις ἠπίστατο τὰ τοιαῦτα, ἐν ἀπορρήτῳ καὶ νυκτὸς τοῦ Αἴαντος δράσαντος. θεοῦ οὖν ἦν τὸ ταῦτα διασαφῆσαι, καὶ Ἀθηνᾶς προκηδομένης τοῦ Ὀδυσσέως, διό φησι· (v. 36.)

καὶ πάλαι φύλαξ ἔβην
τῇ σῇ πρόθυμος εἰς ὁδὸν κυνηγίᾳ.

Περὶ δὲ τοῦ θανάτου τοῦ Αἴαντος διαφόρως ἱστορήκασιν. οἱ μὲν γάρ φασιν ὅτι ὑπὸ Πάριδος τρωθεὶς ἦλθεν εἰς τὰς ναῦς αἱμορροῶν· οἱ δὲ ὅτι χρησμὸς ἐδόθη Τρωσὶ πηλὸν κατ' αὐτοῦ βαλεῖν· σιδήρῳ γὰρ οὐκ ἦν τρωτός· καὶ οὕτω τελευτᾷ. οἱ δὲ ὅτι αὐτόχειρ αὐτοῦ γέγονεν, ὧν ἐστι καὶ Σοφοκλῆς. περὶ δὲ τῆς πλευρᾶς, ὅτι μόνην αὐτὴν τρωτὴν εἶχεν, ἱστορεῖ καὶ Πίνδαρος, ὅτι τὸ μὲν σῶμα, ὅπερ ἐκάλυψεν ἡ λεοντῆ, ἄτρωτον ἦν, τὸ δὲ μὴ καλυφθὲν τρωτὸν ἔμεινε.

ΣΟΦΟΚΛΕΟΥΣ ΑΙΑΣ.

ΑΘΗΝΑ.

Ἀεὶ μέν, ὦ παῖ Λαρτίου, δέδορκά σε
πεῖράν τιν' ἐχθρῶν ἁρπάσαι θηρώμενον·
καὶ νῦν ἐπὶ σκηναῖς σε ναυτικαῖς ὁρῶ
Αἴαντος, ἔνθα τάξιν ἐσχάτην ἔχει,
πάλαι κυνηγετοῦντα καὶ μετρούμενον   5

The events of this drama are supposed to commence in the early dawn, the day after that the arms of Achilles had been adjudged to Odysseus. The goddess Athene is seen by the spectators on an elevated place above the stage, called the θεολογεῖον, whilst Odysseus, whom she is intently watching, moves about, sometimes stooping down and looking on the ground as if he were tracking certain footprints, and at other times cautiously approaching the tent-door of Ajax, and looking in through it. Suddenly he hears a very loud voice, which he instantly recognizes to be that of Athene. She tells him that she had been watching his movements for a long time (although he had been all the while perfectly unconscious of her august presence), and asks him for what cause he had been making this diligent search, and says that there is no need of his proceeding with it any further, for that she was ready to give him all the information which he desired.

2. πεῖραν . . . θηρώμενον, "hunting after some attempt upon your enemies, to seize it." This midd. v. generally governs an accus. Cf. El. 1055, καὶ τὸ θηρᾶσθαι κενά. Phil. 1007, ὥς μ' ἐθηράσω.

4. τάξιν ἐσχάτην ἔχει. In Il. 8. 223 and 11. 8 the tent of Ajax is said to have been stationed at one extreme end of the encampment, and that of Achilles at the other, where they had drawn up their ships. The ship and tent of Odysseus stood in the centre. Cf. Iph. Aul. 292.

5. πάλαι κυνηγετοῦντα, "for some time past tracking (or more literally, keenly hunting out) the footsteps" &c. This adv. πάλαι, when joined to a verb or participle in the present tense, expresses an action or condition which was commenced at some indefinite time before, and is con-

6   ΣΟΦΟΚΛΕΟΤΣ

ἴχνη τὰ κείνου νεοχάραχθ', ὅπως ἴδῃς
εἴτ' ἔνδον εἴτ' οὐκ ἔνδον. εὖ δέ σ' ἐκφέρει
κυνὸς Λακαίνης ὥς τις εὔρινος βάσις.
ἔνδον γὰρ ἀνὴρ ἄρτι τυγχάνει, κάρα
στάζων ἱδρῶτι καὶ χέρας ξιφοκτόνους.   10
καί σ' οὐδὲν εἴσω τῆσδε παπταίνειν πύλης
ἔτ' ἔργον ἐστίν, ἐννέπειν δ' ὅτου χάριν
σπουδὴν ἔθου τήνδ', ὡς παρ' εἰδυίας μάθῃς.

ΟΔΥΣΣΕΥΣ.

ὦ φθέγμ' Ἀθάνας φιλτάτης ἐμοὶ θεῶν,
ὡς εὐμαθές σου, κἂν ἄποπτος ᾖς ὅμως,   15

tinued on to the present moment. Cf. vv. 20 and 337.—μετρ., "measuring (with the eyes)," that is, carefully noticing those footmarks of Ajax which were *freshly* imprinted on the sand, as compared with those which were imprinted on it many hours before, when at the beginning of the night he sallied forth from his tent.

7. εἴτ' ἔνδον, εἴτ' οὐκ ἔνδον. Here the inquiry being concerning a matter of fact, οὐκ is the proper negative, whereas in a matter of doubtful speculation μὴ is required. Cf. Sept. Gen. 37. 32, ἐπίγνωθι εἰ χιτὼν τοῦ υἱοῦ σου ἐστὶν, ἢ οὔ.— εὖ δέ σ' ἐκφέρει, "and it (that is, thy hunting) brings thee well out to the end of thy search, as the sagacious step of a Spartan hound." The subject of the former sentence is the proper nominative to the verb.

10. κάρα στάζων κ.τ.λ. It is a general rule of Greek syntax that the parts of the subject which are spoken of as having in them the quality expressed by the verb or adjective are put in the accus. Cf. 366, δεινὸν χέρας.

14—17. ὦ φθέγμ' κ.τ.λ. The voice of Athene, φθέγμα or φώνημα, is the subject of the whole sentence; and the idea seems to be, that the voice is so distinctly Athene's that even without the evidence of sight she is instantly recognized by it.—ξυν., "I apprehend it in my mind whose it is without a moment's hesitation." Sophocles seems to have closely adhered to the epic conception of Athene's unseen companionship with Odysseus. Il. 10. 278, ἥτε μοι αἰεὶ | ἐν πάντεσσι πόνοισι παρίστασαι. Il. 2. 182, ὁ δὲ ξυνέηκε θεᾶς ὄπα φωνησάσης. In Eur. Rh. 575 the same conception is adhered to—

δέσποιν' Ἀθάνα, φθέγματος γὰρ
ᾐσθόμην
τοῦ σοῦ συνήθη γῆρυν· ἐν πόνοισι
γὰρ
παροῦσ' ἀμύνεις τοῖς ἐμοῖς ἀεί
ποτε.

A like conception of a life-long companionship between Artemis, the goddess of chastity, and Hippolytus, is followed out in Eur. Hipp. 84—86—

ΑΙΑΣ. 7

φώνημ' ἀκούω καὶ ξυναρπάζω φρενὶ
χαλκοστόμου κώδωνος ὡς Τυρσηνικῆς.
καὶ νῦν ἐπέγνως εὖ μ' ἐπ' ἀνδρὶ δυσμενεῖ
βάσιν κυκλοῦντ', Αἴαντι τῷ σακεσφόρῳ.
κεῖνον γὰρ, οὐδέν' ἄλλον, ἰχνεύω πάλαι.   20
νυκτὸς γὰρ ἡμᾶς τῆσδε πρᾶγος ἄσκοπον
ἔχει περάνας, εἴπερ εἴργασται τάδε·
ἴσμεν γὰρ οὐδὲν τρανές, ἀλλ' ἀλώμεθα·
κἀγὼ 'θελοντὴς τῷδ' ὑπεζύγην πόνῳ.
ἐφθαρμένας γὰρ ἀρτίως εὑρίσκομεν   25
λείας ἁπάσας καὶ κατηναρισμένας

"To me alone of mortals is this
 grace
Vouchsafed, to share thy company, to hold
Free converse with thee, and
 to hear thy voice,
Though not permitted to behold thy face."—*Potter.*

Throughout the whole of that Play there is not the slightest intimation that Hippolytus was ever permitted to behold the face of his divine patroness.—ἄοπτος is sometimes used affirmatively of a very *conspicuous* object which may be seen at a great distance, but it is never used to express the notion of being "dimly seen." In the only two other places where it is found in Soph., it is used negatively, in the sense of *unseen*, as it is in this place.

18, 19. καὶ νῦν ἐπέγνως εὖ. "And now you well know that I am beating about on the track of an enemy, Ajax the shield-bearer." Ajax is called δυσμενεῖ as a public enemy, and Odysseus was pursuing him, not from any private grudge, but in the public interests.—βάσιν κυκλοῦντ'. Literally, "turning my step about," so as to follow the windings of the track which the foot-prints of Ajax had left on the sand. Cf. An. 225, κ. ἐμαυτόν. Ajax is designated as the shield-bearer, with an evident allusion to the description of his enormous shield in Il. 7. 219, Αἴας δ' ἐγγύθεν ἦλθε φέρων σάκος, ἠΰτε πύργον, | χάλκεον ἑπταβόειον. It was so large that he was easily distinguished by it from all others (Il. 11. 526), and on this account his son received the surname of Εὐρυσάκης, v. 573 *infra*.

20. ἰχνεύω πάλαι. "He is the man, and no other, whom I have been tracking for some time past, and still am engaged in the work." Note on v. 5.

21. νυκτὸς γὰρ ἡμᾶς. "For this very night he has perpetrated *against us* an astonishing deed, if indeed it is he who has done it." The accus. of the person is used when any good or evil is done to him. Matth. Gr. Gr. 415. Cf. v. 109.

ἐκ χειρὸς αὐτοῖς ποιμνίων ἐπιστάταις.
τήνδ' οὖν ἐκείνῳ πᾶς τις αἰτίαν νέμει.
καί μοί τις ὀπτὴρ αὐτὸν εἰσιδὼν μόνοι
πηδῶντα πεδία σὺν νεορράντῳ ξίφει   30
φράζει τε κἀδήλωσεν· εὐθέως δ' ἐγὼ
κατ' ἴχνος ᾄσσω, καὶ τὰ μὲν σημαίνομαι,
τὰ δ' ἐκπέπληγμαι, κοὐκ ἔχω μαθεῖν ὅτου.
καιρὸν δ' ἐφήκεις· πάντα γὰρ τά τ' οὖν πάρος
τά τ' εἰσέπειτα σῇ κυβερνῶμαι χερί.   35

27. αὐτοῖς π. ἐπ. "When a word which expresses accompaniment has αὐτὸς with it, both are put in the dative without σύν." Matth. 405, obs. 3.

30. πηδῶντα πεδία. Much upon the same principle as a cognate accus., the accus. of the way in which one goes is used after verbs of motion. Matth. 409, 4.

32, 33. "And as to some of them (viz. the foot-prints), I assure myself by certain marks, but as to others I am perplexed, and am not able to find out whose they are." τὰ μὲν ... τὰ δὲ are oftentimes used adverbially in the sense of *partly*; but at other times they refer to an antecedent, which in the present case is to be found in ἴχνος. What shows that they are here used as referring to ἴχνια, are not only the verbs σημαίνομαι and ἐκπέπληγμαι, but more especially ὅτου (sc. τὰ ἴχνια). Cf. Xen. Cyr. 5. 5. 23, νῦν ὁρᾷς τοὺς σοὺς φίλους καὶ ἔχοντας καὶ ἄγοντας τὰ μὲν σοὶ (sc. χρήματα), τὰ δ' αὐτοῖς ὑπὸ τὴν σὴν ἀρχήν. The Schol. σημαίνομαι· διὰ σημείων γιγνώσκω.

34, 35. πάντα γὰρ τά τ' οὖν πάρος τά τ' εἰσέπειτα σῇ κυβερνῶμαι χερί. καιρὸν and πάντα are here used as adverbs, Matth. 425. The presence of οὖν in this sentence seems to show that what appears to be a general observation, τά τ' οὖν κ.τ.λ., has a special reference to the present occasion, and that the meaning of it is, "in all things *then*, both in what has already occurred (τά τ' οὖν πάρος), and in what may ensue therefrom (τά τ' εἰσέπειτα), I am guided by thy hand." Accordingly we find that Odysseus acts with great wisdom, first in wisely abstaining from any sort of exultation over his fallen foe, on account of the mad acts which had been already done by him; and again in what ensued therefrom, the self-destruction of Ajax and the altercation about his burial, Odysseus nobly stepped forward, and in a most forcible speech wisely persuaded Agamemnon to grant him an honourable interment. All this wisdom is intended to be considered as the effect of the secret suggestions and inspirations of the ever-present Athene. Il. 8. 36, βουλὴν δ' Ἀργείοις ὑποθησόμεθ', ἥτις ὀνήσει Also Il. 15. 412.

ΑΙΑΣ.

ΑΘΗΝΑ.
έγνων, Ὀδυσσεῦ, καὶ πάλαι φύλαξ ἔβην
τῇ σῇ πρόθυμος εἰς ὁδὸν κυναγίᾳ.
ΟΔΥΣΣΕΥΣ.
ἦ καί, φίλη δέσποινα, πρὸς καιρὸν πονῶ;
ΑΘΗΝΑ.
ὡς ἔστιν ἀνδρὸς τοῦδε τἄργα ταῦτά σοι.
ΟΔΥΣΣΕΥΣ.
καὶ πρὸς τί δυσλόγιστον ᾦδ' ᾖξεν χέρα;   40
ΑΘΗΝΑ.
χόλῳ βαρυνθεὶς τῶν Ἀχιλλείων ὅπλων.
ΟΔΥΣΣΕΥΣ.
τί δῆτα ποίμναις τήνδ' ἐπεμπίπτει βάσιν;
ΑΘΗΝΑ.
δοκῶν ἐν ὑμῖν χεῖρα χραίνεσθαι φόνῳ.
ΟΔΥΣΣΕΥΣ.
ἦ καὶ τὸ βούλευμ ὡς ἐπ' Ἀργείοις τόδ' ἦν;
ΑΘΗΝΑ.
κἂν ἐξέπραξεν εἰ κατημέλησ' ἐγώ.   45

36, 37. τῇ σῇ κυναγίᾳ is the dativus commodi. "And long since have I gone out on thy track a zealous guardian of thee, *for the success of thy hunt.*"

38. ἦ καί is used when some further particular is asked, and seems always to anticipate an affirmative answer. "And is it really so, that I am labouring to good purpose?" Cf. vv. 44. 48, and 97.

39. ὡς ἔστιν ἀνδρός. It is thought by some that ἴσθι is here understood, or in other words, to be supplied by the mind. It is, however, to be borne in mind that the sentence, *as was expected*, is an affirmative answer to the previous question, and may be construed, "yes (sc. πρὸς καιρὸν πονεῖς) since or for (ὡς) these are the works of this man." Cf. v. 98, ὥστ' οὔποτ' Αἴανθ' οἶδ' ἀτιμάσουσ' ἔτι.

40. καὶ πρὸς τί. "And wherefore has he thus violently used his senseless hand?" For the transitive use of this verb, cf. Eur. Or. 1425, αὔραν ... ἀΐσσων.

41. τῶν Ἀχ. ὅπλων, "on account of the arms of Achilles." The genitive with verbs of feeling expresses the cause of that feeling. Il. 16. 546, Δαναῶν κεχολωμένοι ὅσσοι ὅλοντο. Matth. 368.

10   ΣΟΦΟΚΛΕΟΥΣ

ΟΔΥΣΣΕΥΣ.
ποίαισι τόλμαις ταῖσδε καὶ φρενῶν θράσει;
ΑΘΗΝΑ.
νύκτωρ ἐφ᾽ ὑμᾶς δόλιος ὁρμᾶται μόνος.
ΟΔΥΣΣΕΥΣ.
ἦ καὶ παρέστη κἀπὶ τέρμ᾽ ἀφίκετο;
ΑΘΗΝΑ.
καὶ δὴ 'πὶ δισσαῖς ἦν στρατηγίσιν πύλαις.
ΟΔΥΣΣΕΥΣ.
καὶ πῶς ἐπέσχε χεῖρα μαιμῶσαν φόνου;   50
ΑΘΗΝΑ.
ἐγώ σφ᾽ ἀπείργω, δυσφόρους ἐπ᾽ ὄμμασι
γνώμας βαλοῦσα, τῆς ἀνηκέστου χαρᾶς,
καὶ πρός τε ποίμνας ἐκτρέπω σύμμικτά τε
λείας ἄδαστα βουκόλων φρουρήματα·
ἔνθ᾽ ἐσπεσὼν ἔκειρε πολύκερων φόνον   55
κύκλῳ ῥαχίζων· κἀδόκει μὲν ἔσθ᾽ ὅτε
δισσοὺς Ἀτρείδας αὐτόχειρ κτείνειν ἔχων,
ὅτ᾽ ἄλλοτ᾽ ἄλλον ἐμπίτνων στρατηλατῶν.

50. If φόνου is construed as depending on ἐπέσχε, it makes very good sense of the passage, but from its position its dependence on μαιμῶσαν is more probable. Athenaeus adduces from some tragic poet a line which is very similar: ἴσχειν κελεύω χεῖρα διψῶσαν φόνου.

51. δυσφόρους. The Schol. interprets it by παραφόρους, "the *misleading* fancies of his incurable joy." To construe it as some do, the *horrible* or *grievous* or *vexing* fancies of his joy, seems to make the sentence a contradiction in itself; for how could that fancy be grievous to him which was producing in his mind a sense of triumphant joy?

53, 54. σύμμικτά τε λείας ἄδαστα βουκόλων φρουρήματα. Here the adjectives, as it respects the sense, belong to λείας, though as it respects the construction they are joined to φρουρήματα. We may construe it, "the herdmen's charge of the mingled and undivided spoil." The spoil of cattle was all kept in one place with the spoil of sheep, being not yet apportioned out among the people.

56. κἀδόκει μὲν ἔσθ᾽ ὅτε. The construction is, ἔσθ᾽ ὅτε μὲν Ἀτρείδας κτείνειν ἔχων, (ἔσθ᾽) ὅτε (δὲ) ἄλλοτ᾽ ἄλλον στρατηλατῶν (κτείνειν) ἐμπίτνων.

ΑΙΑΣ.   11

ἐγὼ δὲ φοιτῶντ' ἄνδρα μανιάσιν νόσοις
ὤτρυνον, εἰσέβαλλον εἰς ἕρκη κακά.   60
κἄπειτ' ἐπειδὴ τοῦδ' ἐλώφησεν πόνου,
τοὺς ζῶντας αὖ δεσμοῖσι συνδήσας βοῶν
ποίμνας τε πάσας ἐς δόμους κομίζεται,
ὡς ἄνδρας, οὐχ ὡς εὐκερων ἄγραν ἔχων.
καὶ νῦν κατ' οἴκους συνδέτους αἰκίζεται.   65
δείξω δὲ καὶ σοὶ τήνδε περιφανῆ νόσον,
ὡς πᾶσιν Ἀργείοισιν εἰσιδὼν θροῇς.
θαρσῶν δὲ μίμνε μηδὲ συμφορὰν δέχου
τὸν ἄνδρ'· ἐγὼ γὰρ ὀμμάτων ἀποστρόφους
αὐγὰς ἀπείρξω σὴν πρόσοψιν εἰσιδεῖν.   70
οὗτος, σὲ τὸν τὰς αἰχμαλωτίδας χέρας
δεσμοῖς ἀπευθύνοντα προσμολεῖν καλῶ·
Αἴαντα φωνῶ· στεῖχε δωμάτων πάρος.

ΟΔΥΣΣΕΥΣ.
τί δρᾷς, Ἀθάνα; μηδαμῶς σφ' ἔξω κάλει.

ΑΘΗΝΑ.
οὐ σῖγ' ἀνέξει μηδὲ δειλίαν ἀρεῖς;   75

66. δείξω δὲ καὶ σοὶ τήνδε περιφανῆ νόσον. περιφανῆ appears to be proleptic in the same manner as ἀποστρόφους is in v. 69. "I will show you this disease so as to make it manifest to you." "The adjective often contains not a definition in itself belonging to the substantive, but an extension of the idea contained in the verb, or it may be considered as the consequence and effect of the verb." Matth. 446, 10, obs. 2. Cf. v. 81.
72. ἀπευθύνοντα seems to be literally, to rule, that is, to control or bind the hands with cords. O. T. 104.
75. οὐ σῖγ' ἀνέξει; σῖγα being an adverb, the literal translation of this phrase would seem to be, "will you not *endure* or *patiently remain* in silence?" Od. 4. 595, ἐγὼ παρὰ σοί γ' ἀνεχοίμην ἥμενος, "I could bear to stay with you," or in more complimentary phrase, "I could agreeably prolong my stay with you." οὐ is common to both members of the sentence; for if, as Matth. 498. c. observes, μηδὲ δειλίαν ἀρεῖς is equivalent to καὶ ἄλκιμος ἔσει, it is plain that the latter phrase being substituted for it would be governed by οὐ. We may construe the sentence, "Will you not keep silence and suppress your fears?" Cf. O. T. 637.

ΟΔΥΣΣΕΥΣ.
μὴ πρὸς θεῶν· ἀλλ' ἔνδον ἀρκείτω μένων.
ΑΘΗΝΑ.
τί μὴ γένηται; πρόσθεν οὐκ ἀνὴρ ὅδ' ἦν;
ΟΔΥΣΣΕΥΣ.
ἐχθρός γε τῷδε τἀνδρὶ καὶ τανῦν ἔτι.
ΑΘΗΝΑ.
οὔκουν γέλως ἥδιστος εἰς ἐχθροὺς γελᾶν;
ΟΔΥΣΣΕΥΣ.
ἐμοὶ μὲν ἀρκεῖ τοῦτον ἐν δόμοις μένειν. 80
ΑΘΗΝΑ.
μεμηνότ' ἄνδρα περιφανῶς ὀκνεῖς ἰδεῖν;
ΟΔΥΣΣΕΥΣ.
φρονοῦντα γάρ νιν οὐκ ἂν ἐξέστην ὄκνῳ.
ΑΘΗΝΑ.
ἀλλ' οὐδὲ νῦν σε μὴ παρόντ' ἴδῃ πέλας.

77. τί μὴ γένηται; "lest what should happen?" This refers back to what Odysseus had just said, most earnestly imploring Athene not to call Ajax out. Cf. 107, πρὶν ἂν τί δράσῃς; "before you do what?" which also refers back to the previous words.—πρόσθεν οὐκ ἀνὴρ ὅδ' ἦν; "Was he not a man before?" Various attempts have been made to explain this brief interrogative sentence, by way of showing if possible that it contains a sensible and wise remark. But it was never intended to do so. Mr. Jebb rightly observes, that "Athene affects to ignore the difference between Ajax mad and Ajax sane." Her argument was this: "If he was a man even a mighty warrior before he became mad, and you did not fear being confronted with him then, why should you fear him now?" Her object in putting such a foolish question as this to Odysseus was simply to elicit from him a reply, such as a wise man was likely to return to her (the Schol. ἔμφρονος γὰρ ἦν τὸ τῷ μεμηνότι παραχωρεῖν); and therefore as soon as she had drawn from him the reply (82), "I would not have shunned him even now but for his madness," Athene at once proceeds to quiet his reasonable fear by the promise of her divine aid—"I will darken his eyes, that he shall not see you." Ajax is then brought on the stage, and by a series of questions is led to tell his own tale, and then what may be considered as the prologue to the Play is completed.

ΑΙΑΣ. 13

ΟΔΥΣΣΕΥΣ.
πῶς, εἴπερ ὀφθαλμοῖς γε τοῖς αὐτοῖς ὁρᾷ;
ΑΘΗΝΑ.
ἐγὼ σκοτώσω βλέφαρα καὶ δεδορκότα. 85
ΟΔΥΣΣΕΥΣ.
γένοιτο μέντἂν πᾶν, θεοῦ τεχνωμένου.
ΑΘΗΝΑ.
σίγα νυν ἑστὼς καὶ μέν' ὡς κυρεῖς ἔχων.
ΟΔΥΣΣΕΥΣ.
μένοιμ' ἄν· ἤθελον δ' ἂν ἐκτὸς ὢν τυχεῖν.
ΑΘΗΝΑ.
ὦ οὗτος, Αἴας, δεύτερόν σε προσκαλῶ.
τί βαιὸν οὕτως ἐντρέπει τῆς ξυμμάχου; 90
ΑΙΑΣ.
ὦ χαῖρ' Ἀθάνα, χαῖρε Διογενὲς τέκνον,
ὡς εὖ παρέστης· καί σε παγχρύσοις ἐγὼ
στέψω λαφύροις τῆσδε τῆς ἄγρας χάριν.
ΑΘΗΝΑ.
καλῶς ἔλεξας. ἀλλ' ἐκεῖνό μοι φράσον,
ἔβαψας ἔγχος εὖ πρὸς Ἀργείων στρατῷ; 95
ΑΙΑΣ.
κόμπος πάρεστι κοὐκ ἀπαρνοῦμαι τὸ μή.
ΑΘΗΝΑ.
ἦ καὶ πρὸς Ἀτρείδαισιν ᾔχμασας χέρα;

87. σίγα νυν ἑστὼς καὶ μέν' ὡς κυρεῖς ἔχων. "Standing then silent remain even just as you are."—ἔχειν when joined to an adverb always signifies, *to be* in the state which the adverb expresses. This is the case also with those adverbs, ὡς, οὕτως, ὅπως, ὧδε and others, which refer to some state or condition which is already known. Thus μέν' ὡς κυρεῖς ἔχων is, "remain in the same state or condition as you *happen to be* in at present."

14 ΣΟΦΟΚΛΕΟΥΣ

ΑΙΑΣ.
ὥστ' οὔποτ' Αἴανθ' οἵδ' ἀτιμάσουσ' ἔτι.

ΑΘΗΝΑ.
τεθνᾶσιν ἄνδρες, ὡς τὸ σὸν ξυνῆκ' ἐγώ.

ΑΙΑΣ.
θανόντες ἤδη τἄμ' ἀφαιρείσθων ὅπλα.   100

ΑΘΗΝΑ.
εἶεν, τί γὰρ δὴ παῖς ὁ τοῦ Λαερτίου,
ποῦ σοι τύχης ἕστηκεν; ἦ πέφευγέ σε;

ΑΙΑΣ.
ἦ τοὐπίτριπτον κίναδος ἐξήρου μ' ὅπου;

ΑΘΗΝΑ.
ἔγωγ'· Ὀδυσσέα τὸν σὸν ἐνστάτην λέγω.

ΑΙΑΣ.
ἥδιστος, ὦ δέσποινα, δεσμώτης ἔσω   105
θακεῖ· θανεῖν γὰρ αὐτὸν οὔ τί πω θέλω.

101, 102. "Enough of this, but what about the son of Laertius? How has he fared at your hands, or has he altogether escaped you?" εἶεν is used in the case of a transition to a question about another matter.—τί . . . παῖς; Cf. Phil. 421, τί δ' . . . Νέστωρ; The alternative question, ἦ πέφευγέ σε; is put, in case the interrogator is mistaken in the assumption involved in the former one. Elmsley in his note on O. C. 66, ἄρχει τίς αὐτῶν; ἦ 'πὶ τῷ πλήθει λόγις; has collected together a goodly number of such double interrogative sentences, the first in the list being this one of Aj. 102.

106—110. θανεῖν γὰρ αὐτὸν οὔ τί πω θέλω, πρὶν ἂν . . . νῶτα φοινιχθεὶς θάνῃ. This has been said to be an illogical statement. It only becomes such by leaving out of it that which is its most essential part. The full statement is: "I do not wish him to die before the time when he shall die, *having first had his back reddened with the scourge.*" That part which is in italics consists of the participle and its adjuncts, and contains the whole essence and life of the sentence. Wunder compares Phil. 1329 and foll. vv., καὶ παῦλαν ἴσθι κ.τ.λ., which is equally illogical with the statement in Aj. 106—110, if in each case the participle and its adjuncts be omitted. Sometimes the participle contains the main statement, and the verb is only of any importance whatever as introducing it, which is

ΑΘΗΝΑ.
πρὶν ἂν τί δράσῃς ἢ τί κερδάνῃς πλέον;
ΑΙΑΣ.
πρὶν ἂν δεθεὶς πρὸς κίον' ἑρκείου στέγης
ΑΘΗΝΑ.
τί δῆτα τὸν δύστηνον ἐργάσει κακόν;
ΑΙΑΣ.
μάστιγι πρῶτον νῶτα φοινιχθεὶς θάνῃ. 110
ΑΘΗΝΑ.
μὴ δῆτα τὸν δύστηνον ὧδέ γ' αἰκίσῃ.
ΑΙΑΣ.
χαίρειν, Ἀθάνα, τἄλλ' ἐγώ σ' ἐφίεμαι·
κεῖνος δὲ τίσει τήνδε κοὐκ ἄλλην δίκην.

precisely the case both here in Aj. 106—110, and in Phil. 1329—1334.
108. δεθεὶς πρὸς κίον' ἑρκείου στέγης. "Bound to a pillar of the court-surrounded tent," or, to be more explicit, "a pillar of the tent which was surrounded with an enclosed court."—στέγη means a covered dwelling-place, one that is roofed over, and is not open to the sky. It here means the tent of Ajax, as it does in v. 741. The tents of the generals were enclosed within an outer court that was fenced round with palisades. In Il. 24. 448—456 there is a description of the tent of Achilles. It was made of pine-wood, and thatched over with reeds or rushes, or some of the coarser kinds of grass, the ends of which were not shorn off, for the roof is called λαχνήεντ' ὄροφον. The tent of Ajax, we may infer therefore was of a like rude structure —yet at the same time it must have been very spacious to have contained all the cattle which he carried alive into it, 307—10, 346—7, 351—2, 217—220. Such a spacious dwelling-place as this, which may rather be called a wooden house than an ordinary tent, would require wooden pillars to support the transverse beams of the roof. I consider that κίονα στέγης must mean a pillar of the tent or wooden house, because στέγη in all writers appears to mean a covered place. In Sophocles it is used in the sense of a tent, a house, a tomb, or a cavern, but never in the sense of a court, or any other enclosed area that was open to the sky. "Quibus mirum videtur, columnas in tentorio Ajacis fuisse, consulere debent Hom. Iliad. ω. 448." Musgrave.

ΣΟΦΟΚΛΕΟΤΣ

ΑΘΗΝΑ.
σὺ δ' οὖν, ἐπειδὴ τέρψις ἥδε σοι τὸ δρᾶν,
χρῶ χειρί, φείδου μηδὲν ὧνπερ ἐννοεῖς.   115
ΑΙΑΣ.
χωρῶ πρὸς ἔργον· τοῦτό σοι δ' ἐφίεμαι,
τοιάνδ' ἀεί μοι ξύμμαχον παρεστάναι.
ΑΘΗΝΑ.
ὁρᾷς, Ὀδυσσεῦ, τὴν θεῶν ἰσχὺν ὅση;
τούτου τίς ἄν σοι τἀνδρὸς ἢ προνούστερος,
ἢ δρᾶν ἀμείνων ηὑρέθη τὰ καίρια;   120
ΟΔΥΣΣΕΥΣ.
ἐγὼ μὲν οὐδέν' οἶδ'· ἐποικτείρω δέ νιν
δύστηνον ἔμπας, καίπερ ὄντα δυσμενῆ,
ὁθούνεκ' ἄτῃ συγκατέζευκται κακῇ,
οὐδὲν τὸ τούτου μᾶλλον ἢ τοὐμὸν σκοπῶν.
ὁρῶ γὰρ ἡμᾶς οὐδὲν ὄντας ἄλλο πλὴν   125
εἴδωλ' ὅσοιπερ ζῶμεν ἢ κούφην σκιάν.
ΑΘΗΝΑ.
τοιαῦτα τοίνυν εἰσορῶν ὑπέρκοπον

114, 115. σὺ δ' οὖν, ἐπειδὴ τέρψις ἥδε σοι τὸ δρᾶν κ.τ.λ. τὸ δρᾶν is the subject. "Since the doing of it is this delight to you" &c., that is, this delight that you are anticipating. Ajax had said that he would most willingly gratify Athene in anything else, but even to please her he could not forego the very great pleasure he should have in giving his enemy the scourging which he intended. Whereupon she says, "Since the doing of it is this (very great) delight to you, use your hand freely upon him and spare him not in anything that you purpose to do to him." Accordingly Ajax proceeds to his work with the greatest delight, perfectly unconscious of the irony which is contained in what he himself had spoken: τοιάνδ' ἀεί μοι σύμμαχον παρεστάναι.

121—133. Od. expresses commiseration for the calamities of Ajax under a consciousness of the uncertainty of human life. Athene pursues the same train of thought, and counsels him to take warning from Ajax never to speak a proud word to the gods, nor to exalt himself over others whom he might happen to surpass in wealth or power.

ΑΙΑΣ.

μηδέν ποτ' εἴπῃς αὐτὸς ἐς θεοὺς ἔπος,
μηδ' ὄγκον ἄρῃ μηδέν', εἴ τινος πλέον
ἢ χειρὶ βρίθεις ἢ μακροῦ πλούτου βάθει.   130
ὡς ἡμέρα κλίνει τε κἀνάγει πάλιν
ἅπαντα τἀνθρώπεια· τοὺς δὲ σώφρονας
θεοὶ φιλοῦσι καὶ στυγοῦσι τοὺς κακούς.

ΧΟΡΟΣ.

Τελαμώνιε παῖ, τῆς ἀμφιρύτου
Σαλαμῖνος ἔχων βάθρον ἀγχιάλου,   135
σὲ μὲν εὖ πράσσοντ' ἐπιχαίρω·
σὲ δ' ὅταν πληγὴ Διὸς ἢ ζαμενὴς
λόγος ἐκ Δαναῶν κακόθρους ἐπιβῇ,
μέγαν ὄκνον ἔχω καὶ πεφόβημαι
πτηνῆς ὡς ὄμμα πελείας.   140
ὡς καὶ τῆς νῦν φθιμένης νυκτὸς
μεγάλοι θόρυβοι κατέχουσ' ἡμᾶς
ἐπὶ δυσκλείᾳ, σὲ τὸν ἱππομανῆ

144. σὲ τὸν ἱππομανῆ λειμῶν' ἐπιβάντ'. There seems to be a unanimous opinion among all modern editors that ἱππομανῆ belongs to λειμῶνα, and not to σέ; and yet there is a great diversity of opinion about the meaning of this epithet. One says it means a meadow abounding in horses; another, wild with horses; another, over which horses wildly scamper; and another simply, a meadow abounding in grass. Notwithstanding this difficulty that is met with in the application of this epithet to λειμῶν', the opinion of Eustathius and of the older critics whom he seems to have followed, in referring τὸν ἱππ. to σὲ, is by all unhesitatingly condemned, for no other reason than because at this stage of the drama the Chorus did not believe that Ajax was mad. And yet if it be only borne in mind that the Chorus was not here expressing any opinion of his own, but was simply relating to Ajax what others said of him, this apparently invincible objection falls to the ground. "Rumours assail us to your reproach—that you, the madman (as they call you), having entered the meadow have destroyed the cattle" &c. In this translation I have enclosed the words, "as they call you," simply to show that the Chorus repeats the rumour exactly as he heard it, and so tells him the very name by which he was reproachfully designated. If, then, we only view the passage in this light, the rumour which the Chorus

18   ΣΟΦΟΚΛΕΟΥΣ

λειμῶν' ἐπιβάντ' ὀλέσαι Δαναῶν
βοτὰ καὶ λείαν,   145
ἥπερ δορίληπτος ἔτ' ἦν λοιπή,
κτείνοντ' αἴθωνι σιδήρῳ.
τοιούσδε λόγους ψιθύρους πλάσσων
εἰς ὦτα φέρει πᾶσιν Ὀδυσσεύς,
καὶ σφόδρα πείθει. περὶ γὰρ σοῦ νῦν   150
εὔπιστα λέγει, καὶ πᾶς ὁ κλύων
τοῦ λέξαντος χαίρει μᾶλλον
τοῖς σοῖς ἄχεσιν καθυβρίζων.
τῶν γὰρ μεγάλων ψυχῶν ἰεὶς
οὐκ ἂν ἁμάρτοι· κατὰ δ' ἄν τις ἐμοῦ   155
τοιαῦτα λέγων οὐκ ἂν πείθοι.
πρὸς γὰρ τὸν ἔχονθ' ὁ φθόνος ἕρπει.
καίτοι σμικροὶ μεγάλων χωρὶς

faithfully reports becomes an exceedingly probable one; for what could have been more likely to happen than that the Greeks who had seen the wild work which Ajax had done, should at once ascribe it to madness, and reproachfully speak of him as the madman? Certainly he was so designated by them in v. 726 *infra*. Schol. ἱππ.· μεγάλως καὶ σφοδρῶς μαινόμενον καὶ θυμούμενον.

154. τῶν γὰρ μεγάλων ψυχῶν ἰεὶς οὐκ ἂν ἁμάρτοι. "For one who shoots at great persons will not miss his mark." The subject of the verb is sometimes omitted when it is an indeterminate one: in the present case, however, it seems only to be delayed, and is quickly found in the indef. pron. τίς in the following clause. Schol. ἀπὸ κοινοῦ δὲ τὸ τίς. Verbs of aiming or shooting at a mark govern a genitive. Jelf,

506. κατὰ therefore is not required, but in the following clause, κατὰ δ' ἄν τις ἐμοῦ, its presence is necessary. The Scholiast remarks that the language is metaphorical, and that the larger the mark is at which a man shoots his arrow, the less chance is there of his missing it: εἴρηται δ' ἐκ μεταφορᾶς τῶν τοξευόντων. ὅταν γὰρ μείζων ὁ σκοπὸς ᾖ, ἥκιστα τούτου ἀποτυγχάνουσιν.

158, 159. καίτοι σμικροὶ . . . πέλονται. "And yet the small without the great are but an insecure tower of defence;" that is to say, they are an unreliable protection to the state in a time of danger and difficulty without the government of the great.— πύργου ῥῦμα, which is, literally, "a tower's defence," means the defence which a tower affords, and so in fact means the same as a tower of defence. The phrase is here used metaphorically, as

ΑΙΑΣ. 19

σφαλερὸν πύργου ῥῦμα πέλονται·
μετὰ γὰρ μεγάλων βαιὸς ἄριστ' ἂν   160
καὶ μέγας ὀρθοῖθ' ὑπὸ μικροτέρων.
ἀλλ' οὐ δυνατὸν τοὺς ἀνοήτους
τούτων γνώμας προδιδάσκειν.
ὑπὸ τοιούτων ἀνδρῶν θορυβεῖ
χἠμεῖς οὐδὲν σθένομεν πρὸς ταῦτ'   165
ἀπαλέξασθαι σοῦ χωρίς, ἄναξ.
ἀλλ' ὅτε γὰρ δὴ τὸ σὸν ὄμμ' ἀπέδραν,
παταγοῦσιν ἅτε πτηνῶν ἀγέλαι·
μέγαν αἰγυπιὸν δ' ὑποδείσαντες
τάχ' ἂν ἐξαίφνης, εἰ σὺ φανείης,   170
σιγῇ πτήξειαν ἄφωνοι.

πύργος frequently is. Cf. O. T. 1200, θανάτων δ' ἐμᾷ χώρᾳ πύργος ἀνέστας. Eur. Med. 389, ἡμῖν πύργος ἀσφαλής. Also in a line of Alcaeus quoted by Dindorf, ἄνδρες πόληος πύργος ἀρήϊοι, where the brave men that defended the city are themselves called its tower. In fact, the image of a tower is constantly to be met with in the poetry of all nations, to signify protection or defence against an enemy. In the present case the Chorus makes the general observation with a special reference to Ajax, by way of contrasting what the condition of the army would be without him, with what it was when they had among them such a tower of strength as he had always proved himself to be. Od. 11. 556, τοῖος γάρ σφιν πύργος ἀπώλεο.

162, 163. "But it is impossible to teach the foolish people beforehand maxims about these things." The Chorus means to say that it is impossible to bring ignorant and thoughtless people to form a right judgment about matters of state, until they have learned the consequences of their folly by experience.

163. τούτων γνώμας, "opinions or judgments *about* or *concerning* these things."—τούτων is the genitive of the object, in which case it is sometimes found that the English prep. *of* does not well express the proper meaning of it, and we are obliged to use that preposition which more exactly points out the relation of the noun to its genitive. Thus in v. 2, πεῖράν τιν' ἐχθρῶν, "some attempt *upon* thy foes;" v. 1211, δείματος προβολὰ καὶ βελέων, "a defence *against* fear and darts." O. T. 1200, θανάτων πύργος, "a tower of protection *from* the deaths," or a tower of strength *against* them—that is, against the deaths which were occasioned by the Sphinx. Thuc. 7. 57, Δημοσθένους φιλίᾳ καὶ Ἀθηναίων εὐνοίᾳ, "on account of their love *for* Demosthenes, and goodwill *to* the Athenians.'

C 2

20 ΣΟΦΟΚΛΕΟΥΣ

ἤ ῥά σε Ταυροπόλα Διὸς Ἄρτεμις, στρ.
ὢ μεγάλα φάτις, ὢ
μᾶτερ αἰσχύνας ἐμᾶς,
ὥρμασε πανδάμους ἐπὶ βοῦς ἀγελαίας, 175
ἤ πού τινος νίκας ἀκάρπωτον χάριν,
ἤ ῥα κλυτῶν ἐνάρων
ψευσθεῖσα δώροις, εἴτ᾽ ἐλαφηβολίαις,
ἢ χαλκοθώραξ ἤ τιν᾽ Ἐννάλιος

172. The Chorus now begin to express the belief which they really entertained from the first that Ajax is mad, and that it must be some offended god who had driven him on to those acts of folly and violence which he had done. They had expressed such a belief before in v. 137, σὲ δ᾽ ὅταν πληγὴ Διὸς, yet in the previous part of their address they dwelt mainly on the possibility of its being nothing more than the calumnious falsehoods of his enemies. Even to the last the leader of the Chorus still would ascribe the report of his madness to the suggestions of the mighty chiefs, in the very same sentence in which he tells Ajax that he is only kindling into fury his heaven-sent calamity. From the beginning to the end in all that he says about the madness being a false report, the wish was father to the thought.

ib. Ταυροπόλα. The origin of this term is obscure. Cf. Iph. Taur. 1457, Ταυροπόλον θεάν. By a comparison with other compounds of a like kind, οἰοπόλος, αἰπόλος, ὑοπόλος, ἱπποπόλος, βουπόλος, its meaning may be inferred to be, one who had the management of bulls in some way or other. By some it is supposed that this goddess is so called because she was worshipped at Tauris.

177, 178. ἤ ῥα κλυτῶν ἐνάρων ψευσθεῖσα δώροις, εἴτ᾽ ἐλαφηβολίαις. The two datives, which are only separated from each other by the disjunctive εἴτε, have a common dependence on ψευσθεῖσα, and are datives of the cause: "or else because she has been defrauded on account of the gifts of noble spoils (not being such as they ought to have been), or on account of stag-shooting." It is suggested by the Chorus that the goddess might not have received such gifts, selected out of the general spoils, as she was entitled to for aiding him in a successful war; or that Ajax had offended her by the shooting of stags, an animal that was peculiarly devoted to her service and pleasure. There appears to be an objection to the conj. emend. ψευσθεῖσ᾽ ἀδώροις, which is this: that εἴτε is thus made not to precede all the words of the clause to which it belongs.

179. ἢ χαλκοθώραξ ἤ τιν᾽ Ἐννάλιος. The second disjunctive ἤ is, I think, rightly considered to be a false reading. Among all the various corrections which have been proposed, that of Reiske, namely σοι, seems to be the best. Wunder aptly com-

ΑΙΑΣ. 21

μομφὰν ἔχων ξυνοῦ δορὸς ἐννυχίοις   180
μαχαναῖς ἐτίσατο λώβαν;
οὔ ποτε γὰρ φρενόθεν γ' ἐπ' ἀριστερὰ,   ἀντ.   183
παῖ Τελαμῶνος, ἔβας
τόσσον ἐν ποίμναις πίτνων·   185
ἤκοι γὰρ ἂν θεία νόσος· ἀλλ' ἀπερύκοι
καὶ Ζεὺς κακὰν καὶ Φοῖβος Ἀργείων φάτιν.
εἰ δ' ὑποβαλλόμενοι
κλέπτουσι μύθους οἱ μεγάλοι βασιλῆς,
ἢ τᾶς ἀσώτου Σισυφιδᾶν γενεᾶς,   190
μὴ μή μ', ἄναξ, ἔθ' ὧδ' ἐφάλοις κλισίαις
ὄμμ' ἔχων κακὰν φάτιν ἄρῃ.   193
ἀλλ' ἄνα ἐξ ἑδράνων, ὅπου μακραίωνι   ἐπῳδ.

pares it with Eur. Or. 1069, ἓν μὲν πρῶτά σοι μομφὴν ἔχω, and Phoen. 773, ὥστε μοι μομφὰς ἔχειν.
180. ἐννυχίοις μαχαναῖς. "Or has Enyalios of the brazen breastplate, having some complaint against you for your disregard of his aiding spear, avenged the insult by means of the devices of the night?" It is here implied that the device, which Ajax had conceived and endeavoured to carry out by night, was secretly suggested to him by Enyalios. μηχανὴ signifies a *device*, a *plot*, or *contrivance*. Be it observed, then, that ἐννυχίοις μηχαναῖς means the device itself, in whatsoever way the thought of it came into the mind of Ajax, and not the suggestion of the thought.
191. μὴ μή . . . ἐφάλοις κλισίαις ὄμμ' ἔχων κ.τ.λ. "Do not, do not, O king, by keeping thine eye any longer thus (wildly or intently, ὧδε) fixed on the seashore tents, raise up an evil report against yourself."—κλισίαις is a dative of direction. "The idea of direction lies at the foundation of the use of the dative." Matth. The only difference between ὄμμ' ἔχων and ὄμμ' ἐπέχων is, that ἐπὶ in composition with ἔχων would tend to mark the idea of direction more precisely. Matth. 402. Cf. v. 240. Ajax keeps his eye intently fixed on the distant tents, being, as it seems, still under the delusion that he had slain those inmates of them whom he looked upon as his deadliest foes.
194, 195. ἀλλ' ἄνα . . . ἀγωνίῳ σχολᾷ. "But arise from thy seat, wheresoever thou art fixed in this long-continued troublous rest."—ἀγωνίῳ σχ. is a very remarkable expression, and may be compared with a somewhat similar one in Horace—"strenua nos exercet inertia." Its literal meaning is "a struggling rest." It intimates that there was a violent struggling in his mind with the wildest passions, as is evident from what follows:

22 ΣΟΦΟΚΛΕΟΥΣ

στηρίζει ποτὲ τᾷδ' ἀγωνίῳ σχολᾷ   195
ἄταν οὐρανίαν φλέγων. ἐχθρῶν δ' ὕβρις
ἀτάρβητος ὁρμᾶται
ἐν εὐανέμοις βάσσαις,
ἁπάντων καχαζόντων
γλώσσαις βαρυαλγήτως·
ἐμοὶ δ' ἄχος ἕστακεν.   200

ἄταν οὐρανίαν φλέγων. The Schol. connects the two expressions in the following comment: τὴν ἐκ τοῦ οὐρανοῦ πεμφθεῖσαν ἄτην αὔξων, καὶ οἷον ἐμπυρούμενος ὑπὸ τοῦ πάθους καὶ ἐν ἀγωνίᾳ πολλῇ ὤν. So Dind.: "ἀγωνίῳ σχολᾷ recte interpretantur qui otium intelligunt contentionis et discriminis plenum, et sic fere scholiasta, τὸν ἀγῶνα ἐμποιοῦντα σοί." So Erfurdt: "ἀγώνιος σχολὴ h. l. est molestum otium." So Brunck and Camerarius: "hac anxia mora."—The usual way of construing this phrase is, "a cessation from war," or as L. and S. render it, "a rest from combat." But how could Ajax be said to have abstained from any combat with the Trojans for a long time, by merely sitting still in one place for a few hours? Yet this might well be called a long time for him to remain fixed as a motionless statue in one place, and to keep his eye fixed in one direction, labouring all the while with the most violent passions that raged within him.—ἄνα being a contraction for ἀνάστηθι, requires to be fully pronounced. It suffers, therefore, no elision when the following word begins with a vowel.—ὅπου ... ποτέ, "wheresoever it be." The Chorus was addressing the absent son of Telamon, and consequently was ignorant of the exact place in the tent where he was sitting.

196. ἄταν οὐρανίαν. What is this "heaven-sent calamity" but his madness? It is always spoken of as a direct infliction from some god. Hence it is called in v. 137 πληγὴ Διὸς, and in v. 186 θεία νόσος. Hence the Chorus, not knowing that Athene had cast this madness on him, questions whether it might not have been inflicted on him by Artemis or Enyalios. Be it observed that the space of time in which Ajax is said to have been inflaming the fury of his heaven-sent calamity, synchronizes with that in which he is said to have remained fixed as a motionless statue in an agonizing rest; and yet the madness had only seized him on the previous night. The sense of the passage is expressed in the following metrical translation:

"Rise from thy seat, O king,
    where all too long
In lingering anguish thou hast
    borne the wrong,
Feeding the wrathful curse of
    Heaven."—*Dale.*

196—200. ἐχθρῶν δ' ὕβρις ... ἕστακε. "But the scoffing of your enemies fearlessly speeds along in the sheltered vales, all of them clattering with their

ΑΙΑΣ. 23

ΤΕΚΜΗΣΣΑ.
ναὸς ἀρωγοὶ τῆς Αἴαντος,
γενεᾶς χθονίων ἀπ' Ἐρεχθειδῶν,
ἔχομεν στοναχὰς οἱ κηδόμενοι
τοῦ Τελαμῶνος τηλόθεν οἴκου.
νῦν γὰρ ὁ δεινὸς μέγας ὠμοκρατὴς   205
Αἴας θολερῷ
κεῖται χειμῶνι νοσήσας.
ΧΟΡΟΣ.
τί δ' ἐνήλλακται τῆς ἀμερίας

tongues in bitter railing, whilst on me grief has infixed itself."— ἔστακε stands opposed to ὁρμᾶται. The insolence of the one party has free course, whilst the grief occasioned by it in the other stands fixed and unchanged. The wooded glens seem to be the same as the λειμῶνα in v. 144, where Ajax had slain the cattle. Thither would all the Greeks flock together to see and hear about the mischief which Ajax had done. These glens were said to be well favoured with respect to the winds, that is, they were sheltered from them, and so both for pasture and shelter they were well suited for the keeping of the herds and flocks which belonged to the whole army. Cf. Eur. And. 747. 201—207. ναὸς ἀρωγοὶ . . . νοσήσας. "O ye assistant mariners of the ship of Ajax, sprung from the earth-born Erechthidae, we who are distressed for the far-off house of Telamon are pouring out our lamentations; for now the terrible, the huge, the strong-shouldered Ajax lies disordered with a turbid storm." The Salaminians are identified with the Athenians with respect to their origin. One of the first kings of Athens was Erechtheus, son of Pandion, or according to another myth, the son of Vulcan and the Earth.—ἔχομεν here in conjunction with στοναχὰς expresses a continuous sound, as in v. 319 γόους ἔχειν; see L. and S. under the v. ἔχειν, 2. 10.—ὁ δεινὸς μέγ. ὠμ. Herm. rightly observes that the article belongs to the two follg. epithets as much as it does to δεινός. μέγας is used literally for *great in stature*, and so it suits well the other epithet descriptive of his person, ὠμοκρατὴς, "strong-shouldered." So these two things are put together in the personal description of him in Il. 3. 226.—θολερῷ χειμῶνι well represents that turbid storm which was troubling his inmost soul, and is alluded to in that remarkable expression, ἀγωνίῳ σχολᾷ.

208, 209. τί δ' ἐνήλλακται . . . βάρος; "By what heavy calamity has the night, which is just passed away, been changed in its condition from the day which preceded it?"—τῆς ἡμερίας is the same as τῆς ἡμ. ὥρας, "the time of day-light," and so ἡ πρωΐα and ἡ ἑωθινὴ, where ὥρα requires to be understood.

ΣΟΦΟΚΛΕΟΥΣ

νὺξ ἥδε βάρος ;
παῖ τοῦ Φρυγίοιο Τελεύταντος,   210
λέγ', ἐπεί σε λέχος δουριάλωτον
στέρξας ἀνέχει θούριος Αἴας·
ὥστ' οὐκ ἂν ἄϊδρις ὑπείποις.

ΤΕΚΜΗΣΣΑ.
πῶς δῆτα λέγω λόγον ἄρρητον ;
θανάτῳ γὰρ ἴσον βάρος ἐκπεύσει.   215
μανίᾳ γὰρ ἁλοὺς ἡμῖν ὁ κλεινὸς

210—212. Teleutas was a king of Phrygia, who was slain in war by Ajax, and the young princess his daughter became the spear-won property of the conqueror. The comp. ἀνέχει here in connexion with the participle expresses the idea of continuance—" he constantly loves thee." So the same idea is expressed in O. C. 674, τὸν οἰνῶπ' ἀνέχουσα κισσόν ; and Herm. in his note on that verse quotes Aristides, vol. i. p. 19, καὶ τῶν ἀνθρώπων ὅσοι θεοφιλεῖς, οὐκ "Ἀτη πατεῖ τὰς κεφαλὰς, Ἀθηνᾶ δὲ ἀνέχει καὶ ἐμβατεύει. In the intransitive use of this verb the same idea of continuance is retained. Thus λόγος ἔχει, "there is a report ;" λόγος κατέχει, "a report prevails ;" but λόγος ἀνέχει, O. C. 1573, is "a story holds on continually," or "the story is constantly maintained." So above in v. 75, οὐ σῖγ' ἀνέξει; "will you not continue silent ?"

214—217. The MSS. vary between πάθος and βάρος, but inasmuch as the Chorus had asked Tecmessa about the βάρος which had come upon them during the last night, it would be natural for her to repeat the word, and to say, "You will hear of a βάρος which is equal to death.".

216. ἡμῖν ὁ κλεινὸς νύκτερος Αἴας ἀπελωβήθη. The position of νύκτερος ought to show beyond all manner of doubt that it is a descriptive epithet of Αἴας, and that the article belongs to it as much as it does to κλεινός. Both these epithets require to be taken in a bad sense, and it is necessary to suppose that Tecmessa utters them in a sorrowful tone, as one who believes that Ajax will henceforth be known and spoken of as ὁ νύκτερος Αἴας, "the notorious man of night," because he had gone out stealthily by night and slain the cattle. We may construe it, " for seized with madness our famous night-marauding Ajax is utterly disgraced." In this way the sentence becomes more natural and lifelike; for in all cases where the feelings are wrought up to a high pitch, the mind seeks out for novel expressions of the strongest and most emphatic kind. νύκτερος is the most emphatic word in the sentence. With respect to κλεινὸς being taken in a bad sense comp. Elect. 300, where it is used of a man who had become famous or notorious only by his evil deeds.

ΑΙΑΣ. 25

νύκτερος Αἴας ἀπελωβήθη.
τοιαῦτ' ἂν ἴδοις σκηνῆς ἔνδον
χειροδάϊκτα σφάγι' αἱμοβαφῆ,
κείνου χρηστήρια τἀνδρός.   220

ΧΟΡΟΣ.
οἵαν ἐδήλωσας ἀνδρὸς αἴθονος ἀγγελίαν ἄτλατον οὐδὲ
    φευκτάν,   στρ.
τῶν μεγάλων Δαναῶν ὕπο κληζομέναν,   225
τὰν ὁ μέγας μῦθος ἀέξει.
οἴμοι φοβοῦμαι τὸ προσέρπον. περίφαντος ἀνὴρ
θανεῖται παραπλήκτῳ χερί, συγκατακτὰς   230
κελαινοῖς ξίφεσιν βοτὰ καὶ βοτῆρας ἱππονόμους.

229—231. "Alas! I fear what is coming: the man will evidently die by his own mad hand, having already slain both the herds and the horse-keeping herdsmen with his dark sword." περίφαντος is here used in the same way as δῆλος and φανερὸς sometimes are. Cf. 326, καὶ δῆλός ἐστιν ὥς τι δρασείων κακόν. Also Xen. An. 2. 6. 23, στέργων δὲ φανερὸς μὲν ἦν οὐδένα, ὅτῳ δὲ φαίη φίλος εἶναι, ἔνδηλος ἐγίγνετο ἐπιβουλεύων. The Schol. φανερὸς παραπλήκτῳ χερὶ θανεῖται. ἤγουν διὰ τῆς αὐτοῦ ἰδίας χειρὸς τῆς μανικῆς. Brunck, Herm., Dind., and others take the same view of it. Indeed this method of construing the passage is so obvious that no critic that I am aware of has ever brought any objection against it on grammatical grounds. The only objection which has been brought against it has no relevancy whatever to the construction of the passage; but it is thought that the Chorus at this stage of the drama could have had no possible reason for fearing that Ajax would destroy himself: but most people, I think, will agree with the Scholiast that there was good reason to fear that one so deranged as he was would destroy himself: εἰκὸς γὰρ τὸν νοῦ ἐξεστηκότα μηδὲ ἑαυτοῦ ἀνασχέσθαι. He therefore added, φανερός ἐστιν ὅτι ταῦτα ἑαυτὸν διαθήσει. In the agitation of his mind the Chorus afterwards expressed a fear (v. 254) that Ajax and his friends would be stoned to death. All this is very natural—that fears of a different kind should arise in the same mind at different times, when new circumstances have arisen that might reasonably excite new fears.

231. βοτῆρας ἱππονόμους, "horse-keeping herdsmen." In Eur. Phoen. we find that the same herdsmen which in v. 25 are called βουκόλοι, are called ἱπποβουκόλοι in v. 28. Perhaps it may mean that they were herdsmen who kept horses for their own use in visiting the more distant parts of their cattle-

ΣΟΦΟΚΛΕΟΥΣ

ΤΕΚΜΗΣΣΑ.

ὤμοι· κεῖθεν κεῖθεν ἄρ' ἡμῖν 233
δεσμῶτιν ἄγων ἤλυθε ποίμναν·
ὧν τὰ μὲν εἴσω 'σφαζ' ἐπὶ γαίας, 235
τὰ δὲ πλευροκοπῶν δίχ' ἀνερρήγνυ.
δύο δ' ἀργίποδας κριοὺς ἀνελὼν
τοῦ μὲν κεφαλὴν καὶ γλῶσσαν ἄκραν
ῥίπτει θερίσας, τὸν δ' ὀρθὸν ἄνω
κίονι δήσας 240
μέγαν ἱπποδέτην ῥυτῆρα λαβὼν
παίει λιγυρᾷ μάστιγι διπλῇ,
κακὰ δεννάζων ῥήμαθ', ἃ δαίμων

station. ἱππονόμους is in most editions of the present day set aside for ἱππονόμας, which is assumed to mean much the same thing. In the only two places where the latter word is met with, namely, Eur. Hipp. 1399, and Aristoph. Nub. 571, it means a charioteer. The metrical objection to ἱππονόμους is discussed in the Appendix on vv. 600—608.

235, 236. ὧν τὰ μὲν ... ἀνερρήγνυ. "Of whom some he laid on the ground, and cut their throats, and others, striking them on their sides, he cleft asunder." Another reading, τὴν μὲν, is adopted by some editors. τὰ μὲν ... τὰ δὲ is the usual formula; but whether anything like τὴν μὲν ... τὰ δὲ can be met with in any Greek writer, referring back, as this appears to do, to a collective noun, such as ποίμνην, is, I think, extremely doubtful.

240. κίονι δήσας. Mr. Jebb says, "κίονι, 'at a pillar' (local dative): not 'to a pillar.'" If this were a right exegesis, κίονι would have nothing to do with the action of the verb, and the mention of it would be worse than useless. It would be a troublesome impertinence; for if the pillar were only mentioned to tell us that the animal was not bound to it, the mention of it would serve no other purpose than to perplex the mind, how the animal could in that case be kept in an erect posture. A reference, however, to v. 108, where the same thing is spoken of, shows that the ram was bound to the pillar, and that δεθεὶς πρὸς κίονα, and κίονι δήσας, are, with respect to the object, only two different forms of expression, meaning exactly the same thing. Cf. Artemid. 1. 68, p. 114, προσδεθεὶς κίονι ἔλαβε πληγὰς πολλάς. The only difference between δεθεὶς and προσδεθεὶς κίονι is, that πρὸς in composition serves to mark the idea of direction more precisely. Matth. 402. Cf. v. 191.

ΑΙΑΣ.

κοὐδεὶς ἀνδρῶν ἐδίδαξεν.

ΧΟΡΟΣ.

ὥρα τιν' ἤδη κάρα καλύμμασι κρυψάμενον ποδοῖν
κλοπὰν ἀρέσθαι,   ἀντ. 245
ἢ θοὸν εἰρεσίας ζυγὸν ἑζόμενον
ποντοπόρῳ ναῒ μεθεῖναι.   250
τοίας ἐρέσσουσιν ἀπειλὰς δικρατεῖς Ἀτρεῖδαι
καθ' ἡμῶν· πεφόβημαι λιθόλευστον Ἄρη
ξυναλγεῖν μετὰ τοῦδε τυπεὶς, τὸν αἶσ' ἄπλατος
ἴσχει.   255

ΤΕΚΜΗΣΣΑ.

οὐκ ἔτι. λαμπρᾶς γὰρ ἄτερ στεροπᾶς   257

245, 246. Hermann's explanation of the word μεθεῖναι is, θοὸν εἰρεσίας ζυγὸν ἑζόμενον ναῒ μεθεῖναι αὐτήν, i. e. τὴν εἰρεσίαν. What makes this explanation more probable is, that whereas it gives to the word its literal meaning, the idea of rowing is a thread of thought which runs even into the next sentence. The Chorus says, "Let us place ourselves on the swift bench of rowing, and let loose the rowing to the ship as quickly as possible; so terrible are the threats which the joint-ruling Atridae are rowing against us." It is so generally understood that the real meaning of ναῒ μεθεῖναι is, to use a nautical phrase, "to give the ship her way" or "to set sail" —this being the required sense —that any inquiry as to the exact meaning of μεθεῖναι might seem to be needless, but it is well in all cases to be able to give the literal rendering. The same thing is differently expressed by Virgil with respect to a whole fleet in Aen.

6. 1, "classique immittit habenas."

254, 255. "I fear a war of stones (or a shower), lest being smitten by it, I share the suffering of it together with this man, whom a terrible affliction holds in its grasp." αἶσα is a destined lot or portion, a word which takes its character of good or bad from the circumstances of the case.

257. οὐκέτι· λαμπρᾶς ... λήγει. This seems to be elliptical. "No longer: for as a rushing south-wind when not accompanied with bright lightning quickly ceases, *so it is with his madness.*"—ὀξὺς requires, I think, to be taken with λήγει. A comparison is intended to be drawn, not only with respect to the fury of the madness of Ajax while it lasted, but with respect also to its sudden cessation. In N. T. Rev. 10. 6, 7, ὅτι χρόνος οὐκέτι ἔσται· ἀλλὰ, the sentence appears to be in like manner elliptical, for in that part of it which follows ἀλλὰ, a principal verb is wanting.

28   ΣΟΦΟΚΛΕΟΥΣ

ᾄξας ὀξὺς νότος ὣς λήγει.
καὶ νῦν φρόνιμος νέον ἄλγος ἔχει.
τὸ γὰρ ἐσλεύσσειν οἰκεῖα πάθη,   260
μηδενὸς ἄλλου παραπράξαντος,
μεγάλας ὀδύνας ὑποτείνει.

ΧΟΡΟΣ.
ἀλλ᾽ εἰ πέπαυται, κάρτ᾽ ἂν εὐτυχεῖν δοκῶ.
φρούδου γὰρ ἤδη τοῦ κακοῦ μείων λόγος.

ΤΕΚΜΗΣΣΑ.
πότερα δ᾽ ἄν, εἰ νέμοι τις αἵρεσιν, λάβοις,   265
φίλους ἀνιῶν αὐτὸς ἡδονὰς ἔχειν,
ἢ κοινὸς ἐν κοινοῖσι λυπεῖσθαι ξυνών;

ΧΟΡΟΣ.
τό τοι διπλάζον, ὦ γύναι, μεῖζον κακόν.

ΤΕΚΜΗΣΣΑ.
ἡμεῖς ἄρ᾽ οὐ νοσοῦντες ἀτώμεσθα νῦν.

260—262. "For the looking on the evils which were his own work, no other having wrongfully done them, suggests to his mind thoughts of bitterest grief." παραπράττειν is to do a thing, contrary to or against orders, law, or right. Cf. Hdt. 5. 48. It may be used concerning any wrong action, but there appears to be no instance of its being used concerning a right one.—μηδ. ἄλλου παρ. is a second predicate of πάθη, the first being οἰκεῖα. The second predicate, as is usually the case, being put negatively, makes the affirmative one more emphatic. So in O. C. 1121, ἐπίσταμαι γὰρ τήνδε σὴν ἐς τάσδε μοι | τέρψιν παρ᾽ ἄλλου μηδενὸς πεφασμένην, where the little word σὴν is the most emphatic one of the whole sentence. —ὑποτείνει, literally, "lays under." Cf. Eur. Or. 915, where it is used of suggestive words of advice. It means, therefore, the laying under his consideration an entirely new subject of grief (νέον ἄλγος), not the intensifying or augmenting of an old one.

269. ἡμεῖς ἄρ᾽ οὐ νοσοῦντες ἀτώμεσθα νῦν. "We, then, who are not diseased are now afflicted." There may be some ambiguity in this brief sentence, for the Chorus did not understand what it meant; but what Tecmessa meant to say is afterwards fully explained by her, and her explanation clearly proves that ἡμεῖς οὐ νοσοῦντες are used of herself in direct contradistinction to Ajax. It is to be carefully observed, that although in her explanation she speaks of Ajax, in v. 274, as being recovered (τῆς νόσου) from the disease of senseless raving madness, yet in

ΑΙΑΣ. 29

ΧΟΡΟΣ.
πῶς τοῦτ' ἔλεξας; οὐ κάτοιδ' ὅπως λέγεις. 270

ΤΕΚΜΗΣΣΑ.
ἀνὴρ ἐκεῖνος, ἡνίκ' ἦν ἐν τῇ νόσῳ,
αὐτὸς μὲν ἥδεθ' οἷσιν εἴχετ' ἐν κακοῖς,
ἡμᾶς δὲ τοὺς φρονοῦντας ἠνία ξυνών·
νῦν δ' ὡς ἔληξε κἀνέπνευσε τῆς νόσου,
κεῖνός τε λύπῃ πᾶς ἐλήλαται κακῇ 275
ἡμεῖς θ' ὁμοίως οὐδὲν ἧσσον ἢ πάρος.
ἆρ' ἔστι ταῦτα δὶς τόσ' ἐξ ἁπλῶν κακά;

ΧΟΡΟΣ.
ξύμφημι δή σοι καὶ δέδοικα μὴ 'κ θεοῦ
πληγή τις ἥκῃ. πῶς γάρ, εἰ πεπαυμένος
μηδέν τι μᾶλλον ἢ νοσῶν εὐφραίνεται; 280

ΤΕΚΜΗΣΣΑ.
ὡς ὧδ' ἐχόντων τῶνδ' ἐπίστασθαί σε χρή.

the very next line she speaks of him in such a way as to show that he was still very far from being restored to a healthy state of mind; and that although she spoke of him in v. 259 as νῦν φρόνιμος, yet in v. 273 she speaks of herself and other friends of Ajax as ἡμᾶς τοὺς φρονοῦντας in most clear contradistinction to Ajax himself. All this goes to show that ἡμεῖς οὐ νοσοῦντες were intended to be as clear a distinction between herself and Ajax, whose mental disease had assumed a new form, as ἡμεῖς οἱ φρονοῦντες were, although he had become φρόνιμος to a certain degree.

274. "But now that he has experienced a cessation and respite from the disease, he is harassed to the utmost with an evil grief, and our trouble likewise is nothing less than it was before. Are not these twice as many evils from being single?" πᾶς ἐλήλαται, "he is wholly carried away;" κακῇ λύπῃ, "with a grief that arises from a bad and disordered state of mind."

278. "I am afraid that a plague from heaven has come upon him." The Chorus reasonably fears that the heaven-sent plague has taken permanent possession of him, because he hears from Tecmessa that a deep gloom has entirely overspread his mind, without the slightest return to his former cheerfulness.

ὅσην κατ' αὐτῶν ὕβριν ἐκτίσαιτ' ἰών
κἄπειτ' ἐπάξας αὖθις ἐς δόμους πάλιν 305
ἔμφρων μόλις πως ξὺν χρόνῳ καθίσταται,
καὶ πλῆρες ἄτης ὡς διοπτεύει στέγος,
παίσας κάρα 'θώϋξεν· ἐν δ' ἐρειπίοις
νεκρῶν ἐρειφθεὶς ἕζετ' ἀρνείου φόνου,
κόμην ἀπρὶξ ὄνυξι συλλαβὼν χερί. 310
καὶ τὸν μὲν ἧστο πλεῖστον ἄφθογγος χρόνον·
ἔπειτ' ἐμοὶ τὰ δείν' ἐπηπείλησ' ἔπη,
εἰ μὴ φανοίην πᾶν τὸ συντυχὸν πάθος,
κἀνήρετ' ἐν τῷ πράγματος κυροῖ ποτέ.
κἀγώ, φίλοι, δείσασα τοὐξειργασμένον 315
ἔλεξα πᾶν ὅσονπερ ἐξηπιστάμην.
ὁ δ' εὐθὺς ἐξῴμωξεν οἰμωγὰς λιγράς,
ἃς οὔποτ' αὐτοῦ πρόσθεν εἰσήκουσ' ἐγώ.
πρὸς γὰρ κακοῦ τε καὶ βαρυψύχου γόους
τοιούσδ' ἀεί ποτ' ἀνδρὸς ἐξηγεῖτ' ἔχειν· 320
ἀλλ' ἀψόφητος ὀξέων κωκυμάτων
ὑπεστέναζε ταῦρος ὡς βρυχώμενος.
νῦν δ' ἐν τοιᾷδε κείμενος κακῇ τύχῃ
ἄσιτος ἀνήρ, ἄποτος, ἐν μέσοις βοτοῖς
σιδηροκμῆσιν ἥσυχος θακεῖ πεσών. 325

συντίθησι δὲ παιδὸς μόρον, literally, "and she puts together the fate of her son." There is much beauty and feeling in the application of the expression to the nightingale. She composes a story about the death of her child. She puts together the notes of her song, blending them in plaintive strains, so as to express her sadness for his loss, and regret for her having cruelly slain him with her own hands.

319, 320. πρὸς γὰρ κακοῦ... ἔχειν. The construction appears to be, ἀεὶ γάρ ποτε ἐξηγεῖτο πρὸς κακοῦ τε καὶ βαρυψύχου (εἶναι) ἀνδρὸς γόους τοιούσδε ἔχειν, "for he always used to say that it was the character of a base and low-spirited man to utter such wailings."—γόους ἔχειν. Cf. 203, ἔχομεν στοναχὰς, and see note.—πρὸς κακοῦ. Cf. 581, οὐ πρὸς ἰατροῦ σοφοῦ θρηνεῖν, and 1071, κακοῦ πρὸς ἀνδρὸς... δικαιοῦν: in both which places ἐστὶν is understood, as εἶναι is here in v. 320.

ΑΙΑΣ.

καὶ δῆλός ἐστιν ὥς τι δρασείων κακόν.
τοιαῦτα γάρ πως καὶ λέγει κὠδύρεται.
ἀλλ᾽, ὦ φίλοι, τούτων γὰρ οὕνεκ᾽ ἐστάλην,
ἀρήξατ᾽ εἰσελθόντες, εἰ δύνασθέ τι.
φίλων γὰρ οἱ τοιοίδε νικῶνται φίλοι.   330
ΧΟΡΟΣ.
Τέκμησσα δεινὰ παῖ Τελεύταντος λέγεις
ἡμῖν, τὸν ἄνδρα διαπεφοιβάσθαι κακοῖς.
ΑΙΑΣ.
ἰώ μοί μοι.

330. φίλων γὰρ οἱ τοιοίδε νικῶνται φίλοι. φίλοι is the reading of all the MSS. and scholia. Most editors have adopted the conjecture λόγοις. This makes a difference in the sense. With φίλοι it is, "such friends as he is are won over by their friends." With λόγοις it is, "such persons as Ajax has shown himself to be (who disregarded his own father's parting counsel, and despised the wise suggestions even of Athene herself, 762) are peculiarly accessible to the advice of friends." The repetition φίλων . . . φίλοι is not unusual. Cf. Aii. 73, φίλη μετ᾽ αὐτοῦ κείσομαι φίλου. An. 99, τοῖς φίλοις δ᾽ ὀρθῶς φίλη. Frag. Soph. 92, Schol. Aristidis: καὶ τὸ | φίλου κακῶς πράξαντος ἐκποδὼν φίλοι | Σοφοκλέους ὂν παροιμιῶδές γέγονε. The MSS. reading seems to say, that such as are friends to those who are friends to them are more easily won over to their wishes than such as reciprocate no return of friendliness. It is to be observed that the same form of expression as φίλων νικῶνται, where φίλων is the causal genitive, occurs again in v. 1353;

and to those who know how the same phrase is apt to return to the mind of a writer, it will appear not improbable that the form of expression, φίλων νικώμενος, in v. 1353 came into the mind of the poet in consequence of his having used it not long before in v. 330.

332. διαπεφοιβάσθαι. I cannot do better in this place than take Mr. Jebb's very proper explanation of this word, διαπεφοιβάσθαι; and I do so the more readily, because it is the unbiassed opinion of another person, and at the same time an explanation which has a very important bearing upon what I conceive to be the meaning of the very next sentence which is uttered by the Chorus, in vv. 334, 335, which is the subject of the following note: "'Has been demented by his troubles.' His frenzy has not proved to be a transient malady, followed by a restoration to mental health. He has been taken possession of thoroughly and permanently by an evil influence, which is directing his thoughts to some fresh act of violence."

ΣΟΦΟΚΛΕΟΥΣ

ΤΕΚΜΗΣΣΑ.
τάχ', ὡς ἔοικε, μᾶλλον· ἢ οὐκ ἠκούσατε
Αἴαντος οἵαν τήνδε θωΰσσει βοήν ;   335

ΑΙΑΣ.
ἰώ μοί μοι.

ΧΟΡΟΣ.
ἀνὴρ ἔοικεν ἢ νοσεῖν, ἢ τοῖς πάλαι
νοσήμασι ξυνοῦσι λυπεῖσθαι παρών.

ΑΙΑΣ.
ἰὼ παῖ παῖ.

ΤΕΚΜΗΣΣΑ.
ὤμοι τάλαιν'· Εὐρύσακες, ἀμφὶ σοὶ βοᾷ.   340
τί ποτε μενοινᾷ; ποῦ ποτ' εἶ; τάλαιν' ἐγώ.

ΑΙΑΣ.
Τεῦκρον καλῶ. ποῦ Τεῦκρος; ἦ τὸν εἰσαεὶ
λεηλατήσει χρόνον; ἐγὼ δ' ἀπόλλυμαι.

ΧΟΡΟΣ.
ἀνὴρ φρονεῖν ἔοικεν. ἀλλ' ἀνοίγετε.

337, 338. ἀνὴρ ἔοικεν ... παρών. The meaning of this passage seems to be, "The man seems to be either diseased (that is, with his former senseless madness), or to be harassed with the maladies which have now been with him for some time past," and are still cleaving to him. For πάλαι ξυνοῦσι, cf. v. 5. These maladies, or this malady, that still cleaved to him, and had done so from the time of his recovery from his senseless madness, were mental maladies. They are alluded to just before in v. 332 ; again in v. 345, τάχ' ἄν τιν' αἰδῶ; again more distinctly in 355, ἀφροντίστως ἔχει; and in most express terms in vv. 609—645. Moreover this mental malady is deeply felt and confessed by Ajax himself in vv. 400—402, which made him feel that he was utterly broken down. In consequence of it he was completely overwhelmed with a deep melancholy (κακῇ λύπῃ), from which he never rallied, which totally unfitted him for the business of life, and at length drove him to desperation and suicide.— παρών seems to intensify ξυνοῦσι. Cf. 611, θείᾳ μανίᾳ ξύναυλος, and O. T. 303, οἵᾳ νόσῳ σύνεστιν.

344, 345. ἀνὴρ φρονεῖν ... λάβοι. "The man seems to be sensible—open then the door. Perhaps he will conceive some sense of shame even at the sight

ΑΙΑΣ. 35

τάχ' ἄν τιν' αἰδῶ κἀπ' ἐμοὶ βλέψας λάβοι. 345
ΤΕΚΜΗΣΣΑ.
ἰδοὺ, διοίγω· προσβλέπειν δ' ἔξεστί σοι
τὰ τοῦδε πράγη, καὐτὸς ὡς ἔχων κυρεῖ.
ΑΙΑΣ.
ἰὼ φίλοι ναυβάται, μόνοι ἐμῶν φίλων   στρ. α'. 348
μόνοι ἔτ' ἐμμένοντες ὀρθῷ νόμῳ, 350
ἴδεσθέ μ' οἷον ἄρτι κῦμα φοινίας ὑπὸ ζάλης
ἀμφίδρομον κυκλεῖται.
ΧΟΡΟΣ.
οἴμ' ὡς ἔοικας ὀρθὰ μαρτυρεῖν ἄγαν.
δηλοῖ δὲ τοὔργον ὡς ἀφροντίστως ἔχει. 355

of me."—λάβοι, literally, "he will take up," that is, he will perhaps conceive a sense of shame, which at present he seems to be quite devoid of. This shows that the previous remark, "he seems to be sensible," does not at all imply that he thought him to be perfectly sane; for he would not have added this further remark, "perhaps he will conceive" &c., unless he had looked upon Ajax as evidencing the disordered state of his mind, by the wild manner in which he shouted for Teucer, and by the groans which he uttered. The sense of the passage, as well as the order of the words, unite in showing that ἐπ' ἐμοὶ depends on βλέψας. L. and S. under the word ἐπιβλέπω refer to Dinarch. 99. 22 for ἐπιβλέπειν ἐπί τινι.

348. "O dear sailors, ye alone of all my friends, alone are still adhering to an upright law," that is, in your friendship towards me.

351. "See what a wave encircles me, driven around me from a sea of blood." ἀμφί-δρομον, "flowing around me," depends on φοινίας ὑπὸ ζάλης for the impulsive cause of its motion. Cf. O. T. 1071, ὑπ' ἀγρίας ἄξασα λύπης.

355. δηλοῖ δὲ τοὔργον. "But the work shows how bereft of his mind he is." The whole previous context proves that Ajax is the subject of ἔχει. The previous subject of discussion was the present mental state of Ajax; and when at length the Chorus asks to see him, Tecmessa replies, "Lo! I open the door, and now when you have seen the work which he has done, you may judge for yourself in what state of mind he himself is (καὐτὸς ὡς ἔχων κυρεῖ)." As soon as he has seen him, he exclaims, "Alas! you seem to have given me a report of him which is too true: the work itself shows in what a state of mind he is—he is insane." The report of Ajax which Tecmessa had given him is that of vv. 284—334, which when the Chorus had heard, he came to

ΑΙΑΣ.

ἰὼ γένος ναΐας ἀρωγὸν τέχνας, ἀντ. α.
ὃς ἁλίον ἔβας ἑλίσσων πλάταν,
σέ τοι σέ τοι μόνον δέδορκα ποιμένων ἐπαρκέσοντ'.
ἀλλά με συνδάϊξον. 361

ΧΟΡΟΣ.

εὔφημα φώνει· μὴ κακὸν κακῷ διδοὺς

the conclusion that Ajax must be demented.—οἴμ' ὡς ἔοικας. Cf. 584, οἴμ' ὡς ἀθυμῶ.—ὡς ἔχων κυρεῖ is another form for ὡς ἔχει, and the answer to it is ἀφροντίστως ἔχει. Cf. v. 87.

360. ποιμένων. As all attempts hitherto to explain the meaning of this word have failed of giving any satisfaction, a general belief has prevailed that it is a false reading. Yet by a reference to vv. 600—608, according to the old reading of all the MSS., if only we will accept that reading in what is evidently the drift of it, however much, from the supposed faultiness of its metre, it may appear to have been corrupted, it is as clear as any words can make it that the Chorus were a band of shepherds come from Mount Ida. However ridiculous this may appear to some of those who have never before looked at them in this light, there is nevertheless nothing inconsistent in the notion with the kind of warfare which was carried on by the Greeks in their siege of Troy, according to the traditions which were prevalent in the time of Sophocles and Thucydides of that earlier age. Thuc. I. 11, speaking of the means by which the Greeks were enabled to carry on that protracted siege, tells us that some of them for subsistence betook themselves to tillage in the Chersonesus, and others to predatory excursions. In this very play Teucer is spoken of as having gone for a long time on a predatory excursion to the distant heights of Mysia. If it is spoken of as a matter of history that some of the Greeks went to the Chersonesus to follow a course of agriculture, is it at all less probable that others might go to any place less distant than the Chersonesus, where they might keep flocks of sheep? Sophocles, no doubt, only followed the traditions of his day concerning those mythical times, when the infant Oedipus was cast away on Mount Cithaeron, yet in O. T. 1135 he represents Laius king of Thebes, and Polybus king of Corinth, as having sent their respective shepherds to that distant mountain to pasture their flocks there year after year. Is it not then highly probable that in making the Chorus to consist of shepherds who pastured their flocks in Mount Ida year after year, he only introduced a fiction which was quite in conformity with the traditions of his day concerning the ten long years of the siege of Troy?

362. μὴ κακόν. "Do not by applying one evil as a cure to another make the misery of your

ΑΙΑΣ. 37

ἄκος πλέον το πῆμα τῆς ἄτης τίθει.

ΑΙΑΣ.

ὁρᾷς τὸν θρασὺν, τὸν εὐκάρδιον,   στρ. β'.
τὸν ἐν δαΐοις ἄτρεστον μάχαις,   365
ἐν ἀφόβοις με θηρσὶ δεινὸν χέρας;
οἴμοι γέλωτος, οἷον ὑβρίσθην ἄρα.

ΤΕΚΜΗΣΣΑ.

μὴ, δέσποτ' Αἴας, λίσσομαί σ', αὔδα τάδε.

calamity the greater." This is an answer to what Ajax had just said, με συνδάϊξον. The Chorus says, "Your death, which you seek as a remedy, will only aggravate the misery which falls upon us in consequence of your calamity.—τὸ πῆμα τῆς ἄτης. Cf. Od. 3. 159 and 14. 338; also Phil. 765.

366. ἐν ἀφόβοις με θηρσί. "You see me the daring, the high-spirited one, that was fearless in conflicts with his foes, now showing the terror of his might upon beasts which inspire no fear." The contrast is between the formidable foes whom Ajax was wont to bravely encounter in the field of battle, and the tame cattle which were not formidable to any one. All are agreed upon this point, but the question on which some critics are divided is, whether ἀφόβοις ought to be taken actively or passively. Those who take it passively, "beasts which are unfearedor unfearable," come at once to the right sense of the passage; but those who take it actively come round to the same sense by a circuitous road. They say that beasts which are unfearing are tame cattle, because they suspect no cause for fear, and tame cattle are unformidable; therefore, unfearing beasts are unformidable. But they do not seem to be at all aware that there is a weak place in their argument. The word ἄφοβος never means unfearing or fearless in any such very peculiar sense as they ascribe to it, for it always means fearless in the face of danger, fearless in the sense of intrepid, bold, or courageous. Cf. O. C. 1325; Pind. Isth. 50; Xen. Cyr. 6. 4. 20. But in Plat. Lach. 197 it is thrice used of the boldest and most formidable of wild beasts, the lion, the leopard, and the bear. The only objection which some critics may have to taking ἀφόβοις in its passive sense, seems to be that it is very rarely met with in the passive sense; but if we find it used passively in Aesch. Prom. v. 921, why might it not be used passively by Sophocles? "Mihi ἄφοβοι interpretandum videtur, quos nemo formidat, qui terrorem nullum incutiunt. Sic enim ἔμφυβοι non trepidae sed terribiles, O. C. 39. Apollonides Anthol. p. 73, καί ποτε διηχεῖς ἄφοβος πόρος." Musgrave.

ΣΟΦΟΚΛΕΟΥΣ

ΑΙΑΣ.

ἰὼ γένος ναΐας ἀρωγὸν τέχνας, ἀντ. α'.
ὃς ἁλίον ἔβας ἑλίσσων πλάταν,
σέ τοι σέ τοι μόνον δέδορκα ποιμένων ἐπαρκέσοντ'.
ἀλλά με συνδάϊξον. 361

ΧΟΡΟΣ.

εὔφημα φώνει· μὴ κακὸν κακῷ διδοὺς

the conclusion that Ajax must be demented.—οἴμ' ὡς ἔοικας. Cf. 584, οἴμ' ὡς ἀθυμῶ.—ὡς ἔχων κυρεῖ is another form for ὡς ἔχει, and the answer to it is ἀφρονρίστως ἔχει. Cf. v. 87.

360. ποιμένων. As all attempts hitherto to explain the meaning of this word have failed of giving any satisfaction, a general belief has prevailed that it is a false reading. Yet by a reference to vv. 600—608, according to the old reading of all the MSS., if only we will accept that reading in what is evidently the drift of it, however much, from the supposed faultiness of its metre, it may appear to have been corrupted, it is as clear as any words can make it that the Chorus were a band of shepherds come from Mount Ida. However ridiculous this may appear to some of those who have never before looked at them in this light, there is nevertheless nothing inconsistent in the notion with the kind of warfare which was carried on by the Greeks in their siege of Troy, according to the traditions which were prevalent in the time of Sophocles and Thucydides of that earlier age. Thuc. I. II, speaking of the means by which the Greeks were enabled to carry on that protracted siege, tells us that some of them for subsistence betook themselves to tillage in the Chersonesus, and others to predatory excursions. In this very play Teucer is spoken of as having gone for a long time on a predatory excursion to the distant heights of Mysia. If it is spoken of as a matter of history that some of the Greeks went to the Chersonesus to follow a course of agriculture, is it at all less probable that others might go to any place less distant than the Chersonesus, where they might keep flocks of sheep? Sophocles, no doubt, only followed the traditions of his day concerning those mythical times, when the infant Oedipus was cast away on Mount Cithaeron, yet in O. T. 1135 he represents Laius king of Thebes, and Polybus king of Corinth, as having sent their respective shepherds to that distant mountain to pasture their flocks there year after year. Is it not then highly probable that in making the Chorus to consist of shepherds who pastured their flocks in Mount Ida year after year, he only introduced a fiction which was quite in conformity with the traditions of his day concerning the ten long years of the siege of Troy?

362. μὴ κακόν. "Do not by applying one evil as a cure to another make the misery of your

ἄκος πλέον τὸ πῆμα τῆς ἄτης τίθει.

ΑΙΑΣ.

ὁρᾷς τὸν θρασύν, τὸν εὐκάρδιον,   στρ. β'.
τὸν ἐν δαΐοις ἄτρεστον μάχαις,   365
ἐν ἀφόβοις με θηρσὶ δεινὸν χέρας;
οἴμοι γέλωτος, οἷον ὑβρίσθην ἄρα.

ΤΕΚΜΗΣΣΑ.

μή, δέσποτ' Αἴας, λίσσομαί σ', αὔδα τάδε.

calamity the greater." This is an answer to what Ajax had just said, με συνδάϊξον. The Chorus says, "Your death, which you seek as a remedy, will only aggravate the misery which falls upon us in consequence of your calamity.—τὸ πῆμα τῆς ἄτης. Cf. Od. 3. 159 and 14. 338; also Phil. 765.

366. ἐν ἀφόβοις με θηρσί. "You see me the daring, the high-spirited one, that was fearless in conflicts with his foes, now showing the terror of his might upon beasts which inspire no fear." The contrast is between the formidable foes whom Ajax was wont to bravely encounter in the field of battle, and the tame cattle which were not formidable to any one. All are agreed upon this point, but the question on which some critics are divided is, whether ἀφόβοις ought to be taken actively or passively. Those who take it passively, "beasts which are unfeared or unfearable," come at once to the right sense of the passage; but those who take it actively come round to the same sense by a circuitous road. They say that beasts which are unfearing are tame cattle, because they suspect no cause for fear, and tame cattle are unformidable; therefore, unfearing beasts are unformidable. But they do not seem to be at all aware that there is a weak place in their argument. The word ἄφοβος never means unfearing or fearless in any such very peculiar sense as they ascribe to it, for it always means fearless in the face of danger, fearless in the sense of intrepid, bold, or courageous. Cf. O. C. 1325; Pind. Isth. 50; Xen. Cyr. 6. 4. 20. But in Plat. Lach. 197 it is thrice used of the boldest and most formidable of wild beasts, the lion, the leopard, and the bear. The only objection which some critics may have to taking ἀφόβοις in its passive sense, seems to be that it is very rarely met with in the passive sense; but if we find it used passively in Aesch. Prom. v. 921, why might it not be used passively by Sophocles? "Mihi ἄφοβοι interpretandum videtur, quos nemo formidat, qui terrorem nullum incutiunt. Sic enim ἔμφοβοι non trepidae sed terribiles, O. C. 39. Apollonides Anthol. p. 73, καί ποτε διψήεις ἄφοβος πόρος." Musgrave.

ΣΟΦΟΚΛΕΟΥΣ

ΑΙΑΣ.
οὐκ ἐκτός; οὐκ ἄψορρον ἐκνεμεῖ πόδα;
αἰαῖ αἰαῖ. 370
ΧΟΡΟΣ.
ὦ πρὸς θεῶν ὕπεικε καὶ φρόνησον εὖ.
ΑΙΑΣ.
ὦ δύσμορος, ὃς χερσὶ μὲν μεθῆκα τοὺς ἀλάστορας,
ἐν δ᾽ ἑλίκεσσι βουσὶ καὶ κλυτοῖς πεσὼν αἰπολίοις
ἐρεμνὸν αἷμ᾽ ἔδευσα. 376
ΧΟΡΟΣ.
τί δῆτ᾽ ἂν ἀλγοίης ἐπ᾽ ἐξειργασμένοις;
οὐ γὰρ γένοιτ᾽ ἂν ταῦθ᾽ ὅπως οὐχ ὧδ᾽ ἔχειν.
ΑΙΑΣ.
ἰὼ πάνθ᾽ ὁρῶν, ἁπάντων τ᾽ ἀεὶ   ἀντ. β΄.
κακῶν ὄργανον, τέκνον Λαρτίου, 380
κακοπινέστατόν τ᾽ ἄλημα στρατοῦ,
ἦ που πολὺν γέλωθ᾽ ὑφ᾽ ἡδονῆς ἄγεις.

372. ὃς χερσὶ μέν. It seems almost necessary to take χερσὶ as the dat. of the instrument, "who with my hands *when I had them in my power* I let them go," where we may understand Ajax to say that he did not let them slip from his hands through negligence, but that it was his own act and deed to let them go when he had them in his grasp.

378. This sentence will hardly admit of a literal rendering. The sense of it is, "for these things cannot become otherwise than they are." For ὅπως with an infin. cf. Xen. Hell. 6.2.32, εὕρετο ὅπως μήτε διὰ τὸν πλοῦν ἀνεπιστήμονας εἶναι, μήτε, διὰ τὸ ταῦτα μελετᾶν, βραδύτερόν τι ἀφικέσθαι, "he found out a way how for his men to be neither unskilful" &c.

379—383. "Oh! you prying inquisitor into everybody's affairs, you tool of every mischief, offspring of Lartius—you most filthy vagabond of the whole army—no doubt my misfortunes afford you infinite delight." ἄλημα. This word seems to be nowhere else met with except in v. 390. In An. 320 the Scholiast seems to have read in some copy ἄλημα, but in all extant copies it is λάλημα, which the context evidently proves to be the right word. It is here construed as if it was derived from ἀλάομαι, and is here assumed to mean a vagrant or vagabond, for this suits the character which Odysseus was well able to assume, and in that disguise to practise an imposition on his enemies, for which reason in v. 390 he seems to be called

ΑΙΑΣ. 39

ΧΟΡΟΣ.
ξὺν τῷ θεῷ πᾶς καὶ γελᾷ κὠδύρεται.

ΑΙΑΣ.
ἴδοιμι μήν νιν, καίπερ ὧδ' ἀτώμενος.
ἰὼ μοί μοι.   385

ΤΕΚΜΗΣΣΑ.
μηδὲν μέγ' εἴπῃς· οὐχ ὁρᾷς ἵν' εἶ κακοῦ;

ΑΙΑΣ.
ὦ Ζεῦ, προγόνων προπάτωρ, πῶς ἂν τὸν αἱμυλώτατον,
ἐχθρὸν ἄλημα, τούς τε δισσάρχας ὀλέσας βασιλῆς,
τέλος θάνοιμι καὐτός.   391

ΤΕΚΜΗΣΣΑ.
ὅταν κατεύχῃ ταῦθ', ὁμοῦ κἀμοὶ θανεῖν
εὔχου· τί γὰρ δεῖ ζῆν με σοῦ τεθνηκότος;

ΑΙΑΣ.
ἰὼ σκότος, ἐμὸν φάος,   στρ. γ'.   394
ἔρεβος ὦ φαεννότατον, ὡς ἐμοί,

αἱμυλώτατον ἄλημα. Cf. Od. 4. 245. The epithet attached to it here in v. 381 tends to the same conclusion, for vagrants are usually dressed in ragged and filthy garments, as he is described in Od. 4. 245. L. and S. suppose the meaning of the word to be literally "*fine meal*, and hence metaphor. *a wily knave*." This is a conjecture built on a conjecture, for there appears to be no such word as ἄλημα or ἄλη in use for *fine meal*, whereas ἄλη is in common use for *a wandering*. ἄλημα is used in the sense of ἀλήτης, as λάλημα for λαλητὴς in An. 320.

394, 395. ἰὼ σκότος. "Oh! darkness, my light; O Erebus, most bright thou art to one like me."—ὡς is here used in order more precisely to show that the statement applies only to ἐμοί. Cf. O. C. 20, μακρὰν γὰρ ὡς γέροντι προὔσταλης ὁδόν. This use of ὡς is not confined to the dative. Cf. Phil. 50, πλεῖς δ' ὡς πρὸς οἶκον, where it is difficult to express its precise meaning by any English equivalent. " ὡς πρὸς οἶκον. ὡς ex abundantia additum, ut saepe in hujusmodi locutionibus." Linwood. So in O. C. 15, πύργοι μὲν, οἳ πόλιν στέγουσιν ὡς ἀπ' ὀμμάτων πρόσω. I consider that ὡς is used in a similar manner, and that the right way of construing the passage is, "there are towers in the distance before us, which hide a city from our sight."

ἔλεσθ' ἔλεσθέ μ' οἰκήτορα,
ἔλεσθέ μ'· οὔτε γὰρ θεῶν γένος οὔθ' ἀμερίων
ἔτ' ἄξιος βλέπειν τιν' εἰς ὄνασιν ἀνθρώπων. 400
ἀλλά μ' ἁ Διὸς
ἀλκίμα θεὸς
ὀλέθριον αἰκίζει.
ποῖ τις οὖν φύγοι;

399, 400. οὔτε γὰρ θεῶν γένος. Wunder has rightly explained the construction thus: οὔτε γὰρ εἰς θεῶν γένος; and he has shown that the preposition is sometimes only put after the second noun from An. 367, ποτὲ μὲν κακὸν, ἄλλοτ' ἐπ' ἐσθλὸν ἕρπει. Ibid. 1176, πότερα πατρῴας ἢ πρὸς οἰκείας χερός. "For I am not worthy any longer to look to the gods (in expectation of any aid from them), nor to look for any aid from mortal men."

401—403.
ἀλλά μ' ἁ Διὸς
ἀλκίμα θεὸς
ὀλέθριον αἰκίζει.

"But the mighty goddess sprung from Jove torments me, a ruined man." This word ὀλέθριον is always used in the passive sense, when taken as an epithet of the person; and Ajax here well applies it to himself, for the affliction which had come upon him had utterly broken him down. ὀλέθ. expresses the consequence of αἰκίζει, and so it may be construed, "afflicts me and brings me to utter ruin." The question of metre is discussed in the Appendix on v. 600.

403. ποῖ τις οὖν φύγοι; τις is the speaker himself—"whither can I fly?" According to Dawes's canon, Attic Greek requires ποῖ τις ἂν φύγοι; The cases, however, have been found to be so numerous where ἂν is omitted, that it has come to be considered by all the best scholars to be only a generally observed rule. Ajax says, that if the evidences of his mischievous folly are so apparent, it will be impossible for him to escape the vengeance of the whole army.

404—408.
ποῖ τις οὖν φύγοι;
ποῖ μολὼν μενῶ;
εἰ τὰ μὲν φθίνει,
(- ⏑ -) φίλοι,
τοῖσδ' ὁμοῦ πέλας κ.τ.λ.

The corr. vv. in the antistrophe seem to prove that three syllables have been lost out of the text, between φθίνει and φίλοι, and it is the opinion of many that there is something incomplete in that member of the sentence, which causes to a great degree the acknowledged obscurity of it. There is reason to think that the sense of the whole passage was intended to be as follows: "how can I escape, if those beasts which were left in the field, *together with these that are near to me*, have perished; and if, in consequence of these evidences against me, the whole army will slay me?" If τοῖσδ' or τοῖς δ' ὁμοῦ πέλας, "together with these that are *near* me," may denote the slain beasts that lay aroun

ΑΙΑΣ. 41

ποῖ μολὼν μενῶ;
εἰ τὰ μὲν φθίνει,
(— ⏑ —) φίλοι,
τοῖσδ' ὁμοῦ πέλας,   405
μώραις δ' ἄγραις προσκείμεθα,
πᾶς δὲ στρατὸς δίπαλτος ἄν με
χειρὶ φονεύοι.
            ΤΕΚΜΗΣΣΑ.
ὦ δυστάλαινα, τοιάδ' ἄνδρα χρήσιμον   410
φωνεῖν, ἃ πρόσθεν οὗτος οὐκ ἔτλη ποτ' ἄν.

him, then τὰ μὲν conjoined with the word or words that have dropped out of the text would mean the slain beasts that were *not near* to him, but were afar off in the field where he slew them. Supposing then the actor who personated Ajax to have turned his eye and his hand in the direction of the cattle-field while he spoke that member of the sentence, εἰ τὰ μὲν . . . φθίνει, in its completeness, and then again, when he spoke the words τοῖσδ' ὁμοῦ πέλας, to have turned his eye on the slain beasts that were said to lie around him, we can easily understand how this passage, obscure as it is in its present imperfect state, might have been made perfectly clear to the spectators by the dramatic action of the speaker.—φθίνει, " have perished." See note on v. 1005.

408. στρατὸς δίπαλτος. This may be rendered almost literally, " a double-swayed army," and it seems to refer to the double power of the Atridae, or in other words, to the chief authority and power over the army residing in the two Atridae jointly. Considering what were the hostile feelings of Ajax, as expressed in other places, towards the Atridae, nothing is more natural than that when he spoke of the whole army as being incensed against him, he should speak of it as being urged on against him by them; and the more so, as he had named them before, in vv. 251—253, as preparing a terrible vengeance against him. Then again with respect to the phrase itself, if δίπαλτον ξίφος, Eur. Iph. Taur. 322, means literally a double-swayed sword, or a double-wielded sword, that is, a sword wielded with both hands jointly (and the same may be said of the phrase in Eur. Tro. 1103, δίπαλτον κεραυνοφαὲς πῦρ), it would seem that δίπαλτος στρατὸς would mean an army that was wielded with a double force, and in the present case, the army that was directed in all its movements by the joint power and authority of the two Atridae. It was in consequence of this double power that they are called, v. 251, δικρατεῖς Ἀτρεῖδαι, and v. 390, δισσάρχας βασιλῆς.

411. ἃ πρόσθεν οὗτος οὐκ ἔτλη ποτ' ἄν. "Alas! that a brave man should speak such things as he never before would have endured to utter," that is, would have scorned to utter.

ΣΟΦΟΚΛΕΟΥΣ

ΑΙΑΣ.

ἰὼ πόροι ἁλίρροθοι   ἀντ. γ΄.
πάραλά τ᾽ ἄντρα καὶ νέμος ἐπάκτιον,
πολὺν πολύν με δαρόν τε δὴ
κατείχετ᾽ ἀμφὶ Τροίαν χρόνον· ἀλλ᾽ οὐκ ἔτι μ᾽, οὐκ
ἔτ᾽ ἀμπνοὰς ἔχοντα· τοῦτό τις φρονῶν ἴστω.   416
ὦ Σκαμάνδριοι
γείτονες ῥοαί,
εὔφρονες Ἀργείοις   420
οὐκ ἔτ᾽ ἄνδρα μὴ
τόνδ᾽ ἴδητ᾽, ἔπος
ἐξερέω μέγα,
οἷον οὔτινα

412. ἰὼ πόροι ἁλίρροθοι, "oh! ye pathways of the deep." This phrase is again met with in Aesch. Pers. 369, where it evidently means those pathways or channels of the sea which ships were wont to take. It is not likely that Sophocles should have used it in quite a different sense: that whereas Aeschylus had used it concerning the currents or pathways of the sea, Sophocles should use it as giving a characteristic description of all rivers—namely, that they are streams of water running into the sea.

414—416. In all editions the punctuation is as above, with a full stop after ἴστω, thus making it a complete sentence, and some such word as ἕξετε or καθέξετε is supposed to be understood as governing ἔχοντα. If, however, the whole passage, from πολὺν πολύν down to Ἑλλανίδος, be taken as forming only one complete sentence, it will admit of being construed differently, and as I think, in a better manner, thus: "Ye have detained me a long, long and tedious time about Troas: but *no longer, no longer*, still breathing the vital air (let some one, if she is wise, know this), O ye neighbouring streams of Scamander so propitious to the Argives, *no longer shall ye see this man*, I will speak the proud boast, such a one as Troy never beheld in all the hosts that came from the land of Hellas." Thus the thrice-repeated declaration, *no longer*, before the last word is spoken, which expresses the deliberate purpose of his mind (οὐκέτι με μὴ ἴδητε), adds a force and a pathos to that declaration, which is weakened by the break in the sentence, which the supposed understood word καθέξετε makes in it.—τοῦτό τις φ. ἴ. is specially addressed to Tecmessa by way of preparing her for the execution of his fixed resolve.—οὐ μὴ or οὐ μὴ ἔτι is used with the subjunctive in the sense of the future, El. 42; N. T. Rev. 3. 12.

ΑΙΑΣ.

Τρωία στρατοῦ
δέρχθη, χθονὸς μολόντ' ἀπὸ 425
Ἑλλανίδος· τανῦν δ' ἄτιμος
ὧδε πρόκειμαι.

ΧΟΡΟΣ.

οὔτοι σ' ἀπείργειν, οὐδ' ὅπως ἐῶ λέγειν
ἔχω, κακοῖς τοιοῖσδε συμπεπτωκότα.

ΑΙΑΣ.

αἰαῖ· τίς ἄν ποτ' ᾤεθ' ὧδ' ἐπώνυμον 430
τοὐμὸν ξυνοίσειν ὄνομα τοῖς ἐμοῖς κακοῖς;
νῦν γὰρ πάρεστι καὶ δὶς αἰάζειν ἐμοὶ
καὶ τρίς· τοιούτοις γὰρ κακοῖς ἐντυγχάνω·
ὅτου πατὴρ μὲν τῆσδ' ἀπ' Ἰδαίας χθονὸς
τὰ πρῶτα καλλιστεῖ' ἀριστεύσας στρατοῦ 435
πρὸς οἶκον ἦλθε πᾶσαν εὔκλειαν φέρων.
ἐγὼ δ' ὁ κείνου παῖς, τὸν αὐτὸν ἐς τόπον
Τροίας ἐπελθὼν οὐκ ἐλάσσονι σθένει,
οὐδ' ἔργα μείω χειρὸς ἀρκέσας ἐμῆς,

428. ἔχω is followed with a double construction—first with the infin. ἀπείργειν, and then with ὅπως ἐῶ. "So great are the afflictions that you have fallen into, that I am neither able to keep you from speaking (about them), nor do I know how I can permit it;"—that is to say, "such is my sympathy with your troubles that I am not able to check you in giving utterance to your feelings; yet when I hear you utter words so ominous of your purpose of self-destruction I can hardly bear it." Cf. An. 270.

430. "Alas! who would ever have thought that my name imposed upon me (as with reference to them) would thus accord with my misfortunes? for now it is my fate to utter the lamentation aī, aī, twice and thrice." ἐπώνυμον sometimes means a name imposed on a person for some particular reason.

435. τὰ πρῶτα καλλ. κ.τ.λ., "having obtained by his superior merits the first and fairest rewards of the whole army." The gen. στρατοῦ may either depend on the noun or the participle. Matth. 334.—καλλιστεῖα is a cognate accus. depending on ἀριστεύσας.

439. οὐδ' ἔργα μείω χειρὸς ἀρκέσας ἐμῆς. What may be the precise meaning of ἀρκέσας in

44   ΣΟΦΟΚΛΕΟΥΣ

ἄτιμος Ἀργείοισιν ὧδ᾽ ἀπόλλυμαι.   440
καίτοι τοσοῦτόν γ᾽ ἐξεπίστασθαι δοκῶ,
εἰ ζῶν Ἀχιλλεὺς τῶν ὅπλων τῶν ὧν πέρι
κρίνειν ἔμελλε κράτος ἀριστείας τινί,
οὐκ ἄν τις αὔτ᾽ ἔμαρψεν ἄλλος ἀντ᾽ ἐμοῦ.
νῦν δ᾽ αὔτ᾽ Ἀτρεῖδαι φωτὶ παντουργῷ φρένας   445
ἔπραξαν, ἀνδρὸς τοῦδ᾽ ἀπώσαντες κράτη.
κεἰ μὴ τόδ᾽ ὄμμα καὶ φρένες διάστροφοι
γνώμης ἀπῇξαν τῆς ἐμῆς, οὐκ ἄν ποτε
δίκην κατ᾽ ἄλλου φωτὸς ὧδ᾽ ἐψήφισαν.
νῦν δ᾽ ἡ Διὸς γοργῶπις ἀδάμαστος θεὰ   450

this place it is difficult to define. The Schol. interprets it by three words, which convey three different ideas—δείξας, βοηθήσας, πράξας. Whichever of these may be nearest to its meaning, there cannot be a doubt, I think, that χειρὸς ἐμῆς is a gen. depending on ἔργα—"nor having been helpful with less valorous *deeds of my hand* than he was."

445. νῦν δ᾽ αὔτ᾽ . . . ἔπραξαν. "But now the Atridae have by their machinations procured them (i. e. the arms) for an all-crafty knave, setting aside my valorous deeds."—πράττειν implies some secret intrigue which a man practises in favour of others. It here implies that the Atridae were partisans of Odysseus, and that they so *managed* the affair as to pervert the course of justice. There is a note in Arnold's Thuc. 4. 89 on this peculiar use and meaning of the verb, which is worth attention.

447. "And had not this eye and my mind distorted (by false illusions) strayed from my purpose, they would not have escaped with their lives so as ever again to pass such an unjust sentence against any other man." Ajax expresses his regret that he was prevented from slaying the Atridae by the false illusions which turned his hand against the flocks.

450—452. ἀδάμαστος is the Homeric form; and if the testimony of MSS. is worthy of credit, it is the form which was used by Aesch., Soph., and Eur., except in one or two places in the lyric parts of their plays where the metre may require ἀδάματος. Some MSS. have ἐπεντύνοντ᾽, others ἐπεντείνοντ᾽, or ἐπεκτείνοντ᾽. The former word is used for the preparing of a feast, the harnessing of horses to a chariot, or the dressing of a goddess in the most splendid attire; and in all its other uses as well as in these it seems to express a more careful, slow, deliberate, and complex preparation than the mere arming of a man's hand with a sword. On the other hand, ἐπεκ- or ἐπεντείνοντ᾽ seems to be exactly the most appropriate word which could have

ΑΙΑΣ. 45

ἤδη μ' ἐπ' αὐτοῖς χεῖρ' ἐπεντείνοντ' ἐμὴν
ἔσφηλεν ἐμβαλοῦσα λυσσώδη νόσον,
ὥστ' ἐν τοιοῖσδε χεῖρας αἱμάξαι βοτοῖς·
κεῖνοι δ' ἐπεγγελῶσιν ἐκπεφευγότες,
ἐμοῦ μὲν οὐχ ἑκόντος· εἰ δέ τις θεῶν   455
βλάπτοι, φύγοι τἂν χὠ κακὸς τὸν κρείσσονα.
καὶ νῦν τί χρὴ δρᾶν; ὅστις ἐμφανῶς θεοῖς
ἐχθαίρομαι, μισεῖ δέ μ' Ἑλλήνων στρατός,
ἔχθει δὲ Τροία πᾶσα καὶ πεδία τάδε.
πότερα πρὸς οἴκους, ναυλόχους λιπὼν ἕδρας   460
μόνους τ' Ἀτρείδας, πέλαγος Αἰγαῖον περῶ;
καὶ ποῖον ὄμμα πατρὶ δηλώσω φανεὶς
Τελαμῶνι; πῶς με τλήσεταί ποτ' εἰσιδεῖν
γυμνὸν φανέντα τῶν ἀριστείων ἄτερ,
ὧν αὐτὸς ἔσχε στέφανον εὐκλείας μέγαν;   465
οὐκ ἔστι τοὔργον τλητόν. ἀλλὰ δῆτ' ἰὼν
πρὸς ἔρυμα Τρώων, ξυμπεσὼν μόνος μόνοις
καὶ δρῶν τι χρηστόν, εἶτα λοίσθιον θάνω;
ἀλλ' ὧδέ γ' Ἀτρείδας ἂν εὐφράναιμί που.
οὐκ ἔστι ταῦτα. πεῖρά τις ζητητέα   470
τοιάδ' ἀφ' ἧς γέροντι δηλώσω πατρὶ
μή τοι φύσιν γ' ἄσπλαγχνος ἐκ κείνου γεγώς.
αἰσχρὸν γὰρ ἄνδρα τοῦ μακροῦ χρῄζειν βίου,

been selected for the occasion, and stands well in opposition to ἐμβαλοῦσα. Whilst Ajax is in the very act (ἤδη) of *stretching out his hand* (ἐπεντείνοντ') upon the Atridae, Athene *casts upon him* (ἐμβαλοῦσα) a disordering madness. Hermann informs us that Brunck, Lobeck, and Erfurdt had taken ἐπεντείνοντ', and he adds in his note, "nec sane est quare hoc displiceat." Indeed it is difficult to imagine what objection there can be to this reading.

473, 474. αἰσχρὸν γάρ. These two vv. will admit, I think, of being construed thus: "It is base for a man to desire a long life, because he happens to be one who is in no way cut off from it by calamities." Thus the case of a prosperous man who only desires a long continuance of prosperity, without any higher aim, is contemplated, and not the case of a man who is in a hopeless state of misery. This

46 ΣΟΦΟΚΛΕΟΥΣ

κακοῖσιν ὅστις μηδὲν ἐξαλλάσσεται.
τί γὰρ παρ' ἦμαρ ἡμέρα τέρπειν ἔχει   475
προσθεῖσα κἀναθεῖσα τοῦ γε κατθανεῖν;
οὐκ ἂν πριαίμην οὐδενὸς λόγου βροτῶν
ὅστις κεναῖσιν ἐλπίσιν θερμαίνεται.
ἀλλ' ἢ καλῶς ζῆν, ἢ καλῶς τεθνηκέναι

view of it is in harmony with what follows: "for what has each passing day to delight him, which is only bringing him a step nearer, or setting him off a step farther from the certainty of death at last?" This mention of death seems to be more suited to remind the man of pleasure of the day when all his pleasures shall come to an end, than to caution the poor miserable man, who is already brought down to death's door. It is also in harmony still more with the two next verses which follow the mention of death; for who is it that is warmed with vain hopes and large expectations from the prospect which a long continuance in life holds out to him? Is it the man whose prospects are already utterly blasted and withered to the very root, as those of Ajax were? or is it not rather the man who lives at ease in his possessions, who is exempt from all calamities, and who in consequence of his experience of life hitherto is too apt to think that to-morrow shall be as this day, and much more abounding in all that is pleasurable and joyous? Ajax then does not contemplate the case of a man who lies in a state of hopeless and remediless misery, yet is desiring a long life of it, but rather the case of a man who, having been exempt from calamities hitherto, desires only a continuance of such exemption in a long life of inglorious ease; and he contrasts this low aim of the base-minded with that of the noble-minded, whose prevailing desire is, in whatever state he may be, to live honourably, and when that is no longer possible, to die honourably, which in his view of the matter was to commit suicide.

477. βροτῶν. In all the MSS. but one it is βροτόν. The internal evidence, however, is in favour of that one MS. This word occurs in Soph. more than sixty times, but always in the plural, except in this place. It occurs forty times in the gen. plural. Its use in the gen. plur. in some of those places is very similar to its use in the present instance, as in O. T. 427, σοῦ γὰρ οὐκ ἔστιν βροτῶν ὅστις. O. T. 1194, βροτῶν οὐδένα μακαρίζω ὅστις. O. C. 252, οὐ γὰρ ἴδοις ἂν ἀθρῶν βροτῶν ὅστις. It is true that some metrical critics, under the assumption that the poet intended the end of v. 252 in O. C. to be a dactyl, have changed βροτῶν into βροτόν, while at the same time it has been admitted by others that a comparison of the metre of that verse with several other verses in the same series plainly shows that their assumption was a groundless one.

ΑΙΑΣ. 47

τὸν εὐγενῆ χρή. πάντ' ἀκήκοας λόγον. 480

ΧΟΡΟΣ.

οὐδεὶς ἐρεῖ ποθ' ὡς ὑπόβλητον λόγον,
Αἴας, ἔλεξας, ἀλλὰ τῆς σαυτοῦ φρενός.
παῦσαί γε μέντοι καὶ δὸς ἀνδράσιν φίλοις
γνώμης κρατῆσαι τάσδε φροντίδας μεθείς.

ΤΕΚΜΗΣΣΑ.

ὦ δέσποτ' Αἴας, τῆς ἀναγκαίας τύχης 485
οὐκ ἔστιν οὐδὲν μεῖζον ἀνθρώποις κακόν.
ἐγὼ δ' ἐλευθέρου μὲν ἐξέφυν πατρός,
εἴπερ τινὸς σθένοντος ἐν πλούτῳ Φρυγῶν·
νῦν δ' εἰμὶ δούλη. θεοῖς γὰρ ὧδ' ἔδοξέ που
καὶ σῇ μάλιστα χειρί. τοιγαροῦν, ἐπεὶ 490
τὸ σὸν λέχος ξυνῆλθον, εὖ φρονῶ τὰ σά,
καί σ' ἀντιάζω πρός τ' ἐφεστίου Διὸς
εὐνῆς τε τῆς σῆς, ᾗ συνηλλάχθης ἐμοί,
μή μ' ἀξιώσῃς βάξιν ἀλγεινὴν λαβεῖν
τῶν σῶν ὑπ' ἐχθρῶν, χειρίαν ἀφεὶς τινί. 495
εἰ γὰρ θάνῃς σὺ καὶ τελευτήσας ἀφῇς,

485. ἀναγκαίας τύχης. "There is no greater evil than the doom of an unavoidable calamity."—ἀναγ. τύχ. is an expression which may be used of any great calamity from which there is no escape, and it seems peculiarly fitted to describe the bitter constraint of slavery. It is used concerning the predicted doom of Ajax in 8c3, and of the death of Orestes in El. 48.

494, 495. μή μ' ἀξιώσῃς... χειρίαν ἀφεὶς τινί. "Do not think it right that I should become the subject of scornful reproaches from your enemies, by leaving me in slavish subjection to any one of them."—χειρίαν is a predicate of μέ. Cf. O. C. 1278, ὡς μή μ' ἄτιμον ἀφῇ. An. 887, ἄφετε μόνην ἔρημον (sc. τήνδε τὴν κόρην). El. 1020, οὐ γὰρ δὴ κενὸν γ' ἀφήσομεν (sc. τοὔργον τόδε). There are similar uses of this v. ἀφιέναι having a predicative adjective depending on it in Eur., Hdt., Plat., and, I doubt not, in other Greek writers. On the other hand, I take it for granted that not a single instance can be met with of the v. ἐφιέναι being used in a similar manner; for not one of those editors who have taken the reading χειρίαν ἐφεὶς τινί (merely because it happens to be that of the famous La. MS.) has ever yet been able to adduce a single instance of the kind.

496, 497. εἰ γὰρ θάνῃς σὺ...

48 ΣΟΦΟΚΛΕΟΤΣ

ταύτῃ νόμιζε κἀμὲ τῇ τόθ' ἡμέρᾳ
βίᾳ ξυναρπασθεῖσαν Ἀργείων ὕπο
ξὺν παιδὶ τῷ σῷ δουλίαν ἕξειν τροφήν.
καί τις πικρὸν πρόσφθεγμα δεσποτῶν ἐρεῖ   500
λόγοις ἰάπτων, ἴδετε τὴν ὁμευνέτιν
Αἴαντος, ὃς μέγιστον ἴσχυσε στρατοῦ,
οἵας λατρείας ἀνθ' ὅσου ζήλου τρέφει.
τοιαῦτ' ἐρεῖ τις. κἀμὲ μὲν δαίμων ἐλᾷ,
σοὶ δ' αἰσχρὰ τἄπη ταῦτα καὶ τῷ σῷ γένει.   505
ἀλλ' αἴδεσαι μὲν πατέρα τὸν σὸν ἐν λυγρῷ
γήρᾳ προλείπων, αἴδεσαι δὲ μητέρα
πολλῶν ἐτῶν κληροῦχον, ἥ σε πολλάκις
θεοῖς ἀρᾶται ζῶντα πρὸς δόμους μολεῖν·
οἴκτειρε δ', ὦναξ, παῖδα τὸν σόν, εἰ νέας   510

ἡμέρᾳ. Most MSS. εἰ. Others ἦν, which appears to be the work of former emendators; for in one MS. we find ἦν / εἰ, and in two others εἰ θάνοις. Thus also in v. 521 some MSS. πάθῃ, and others πάθοι, where, however, it is immensely more probable that πάθη should have been corrected into πάθοι, to avoid what was contrary to general Attic usage, than that πάθοι should have been corrected into πάθη. Even in Hermann's time there was no doubt in the minds of the most observant critics that Attic writers sometimes use εἰ with the subjunctive, but since his time the thing has become perfectly well understood (see L. and S. 3, under the word εἰ). With respect to the correction ᾖ, it is to be observed that there is not, I believe, a single instance in the whole of Soph. where when the rel. pron. precedes the noun, the noun is not found in the same clause with it; but, independently of this, ᾖ . . . ταύτῃ, τῇ ἡμέρᾳ is novel and strange, and has certainly nothing at all like it in Sophocles.

510—513. εἰ νέας τροφῆς στερηθεὶς σοῦ διοίσεται μόνος. The right way of construing this passage appears to be as follows: "if deprived of the young nurture he is receiving from you, and being left alone he shall have to pass through it (that is, through the period of his young nurture) under unfeeling guardians." The word τροφή is as often used in a bad sense as a good one. Tecmessa had just before said that if Ajax should die, she herself, together with the child, would have to endure the nurture of slavery (499, δουλίαν τροφήν); and now with respect to the child she expresses a fear of the same thing; for she contrasts the tender nurture which the child was then receiving from his own father, with the harsh nurture

ΑΙΑΣ.

τροφῆς στερηθεὶς σοῦ διοίσεται μόνος
ὑπ' ὀρφανιστῶν μὴ φίλων, ὅσον κακὸν
κείνῳ τε κἀμοὶ τοῦθ', ὅταν θάνῃς, νεμεῖς.
ἐμοὶ γὰρ οὐκ ἔτ' ἐστὶν εἰς ὅ τι βλέπω
πλὴν σοῦ. σὺ γάρ μοι πατρίδ' ᾔστωσας δόρει, 515
καὶ μητέρ' ἄλλη μοῖρα τὸν φύσαντά τε
καθεῖλεν Ἅιδου θανασίμους οἰκήτορας.
τίς δῆτ' ἐμοὶ γένοιτ' ἂν ἀντὶ σοῦ πατρίς;
τίς πλοῦτος; ἐν σοὶ πᾶσ' ἔγωγε σώζομαι.
ἀλλ' ἴσχε κἀμοῦ μνῆστιν. ἀνδρί τοι χρεὼν 520
μνήμην προσεῖναι, τερπνὸν εἴ τί που πάθοι.
χάρις χάριν γάρ ἐστιν ἡ τίκτουσ' ἀεί·
ὅτου δ' ἀπορρεῖ μνῆστις εὖ πεπονθότος,
οὐκ ἂν γένοιτ' ἔθ' οὗτος εὐγενὴς ἀνήρ.

ΧΟΡΟΣ.

Αἴας, ἔχειν σ' ἂν οἶκτον ὡς κἀγὼ φρενὶ 525
θέλοιμ' ἄν· αἰνοίης γὰρ ἂν τὰ τῆσδ' ἔπη.

ΑΙΑΣ.

καὶ κάρτ' ἐπαίνου τεύξεται πρὸς γοῦν ἐμοῦ,
ἐὰν μόνον τὸ ταχθὲν εὖ τολμᾷ τελεῖν.

he would have to suffer under strangers who would treat him no otherwise than a slave. With respect to σοῦ being here used to indicate the person who gives the nurture, compare Elect. 776, μαστῶν ἀποστὰς καὶ τροφῆς ἐμῆς. Lobeck has furnished us with a very apt example of the v. διαφέρομαι being used in an exactly similar way to that in which it is used here, to signify the passing through of a certain period of human life. Hippocr. de Septim. Part. I. 450, T. V. 344, ἄνοσος διατετελεκὼς τὸν χρόνον, ὃν ἐν τῇ μήτρῃ διεφέρετο. Be it observed that σοῦ is emphatic, as σὴν is in O. C. 1121, and is used in a similar way to indicate the author of the gift, and not the receiver.

521. εἴ τί που πάθοι. The optative in the conditional clause is unusual, unless it be answered with an optative in the apodosis. Sometimes the indic. is found answering to it in the apodosis, and more so in general propositions such as v. 521. Cf. An. 1031, τὸ μανθάνειν δ' ἥδιστον εὖ λέγοντος, εἰ κέρδος λέγοι. Trach. 93, ἐπεὶ πύθοιτο, κέρδος ἐμπολᾷ. Also 1344 infra, ἄνδρα δ' οὐ δίκαιον, εἰ θάνοι, βλάπτειν.

50   ΣΟΦΟΚΛΕΟΥΣ

ΤΕΚΜΗΣΣΑ.
ἀλλ', ὦ φιλ Αἴας, πάντ' ἔγωγε πείσομαι.
ΑΙΑΣ.
κόμιζέ νύν μοι παῖδα τὸν ἐμὸν, ὡς ἴδω.   530
ΤΕΚΜΗΣΣΑ.
καὶ μὴν φόβοισί γ' αὐτὸν ἐξελυσάμην.
ΑΙΑΣ.
ἐν τοῖσδε τοῖς κακοῖσιν, ἢ τί μοι λέγεις;
ΤΕΚΜΗΣΣΑ.
μὴ σοί γέ που δύστηνος ἀντήσας θάνοι.
ΑΙΑΣ.
πρέπον γέ τἂν ἦν δαίμονος τοὐμοῦ τόδε.

531. καὶ μὴν φόβοισί γ' αὐτὸν ἐξελυσάμην. καὶ μὴν is so well explained by L. and S., that nothing more need be said. It is a strengthening of the declaration which it introduces, and is used therefore sometimes to call special attention to a fact, as in the case of a new comer. Cf. 539, 794, 1168, 1223; also El. 79, 556, 1045, 1188. "*In truth* I only sent him away through absolute fear;" that is to say, "you shall see him, for I assure you that it was only fear which made me send him away from you."—φόβοισι is a dative expressing the cause of the action of the verb. Cf. O. C. 332, τί δ' ἦλθες; σῇ, πάτερ, προμηθίᾳ. πότερα πόθοισι; also Xen. Cyr. 8. 1. 16, οἱ δὲ μὴ παρεῖεν, τούτους ἡγεῖτο ἢ ἀκρατείᾳ τινὶ, ἢ ἀδικίᾳ, ἢ ἀμελείᾳ ἀπεῖναι.

533. μὴ σοί γέ. The γέ, though it gives a slight emphasis to σοί, expresses an affirmation to the previous question. Ajax had asked her whether she had removed the child through a fear of him at the time when he was in a state of senseless madness (ἐν τοῖσδε τοῖς κακοῖσιν;), to which she replies, "Yes, it was even you, lest he should unhappily fall in your way, and be slain." She hesitated not to tell him this plainly; and so far from his being angry with her, he even commended her for the deed, and the thoughtful-mindedness that she had shown in it. He fully admitted the reasonableness of her fear, and said, "The act of my slaying him would only have been in conformity with my evil genius" (534).—δαίμονος τοὐμοῦ seems to be a genitive of the cause or origin of the supposed act, and admits, I think, of being construed thus: "That indeed would have been a natural result of my evil genius."

ΑΙΑΣ. 51

ΤΕΚΜΗΣΣΑ.
ἀλλ᾽ οὖν ἐγὼ 'φύλαξα τοῦτό γ᾽ ἀρκέσαι. 535
ΑΙΑΣ.
ἐπῄνεσ᾽ ἔργον καὶ πρόνοιαν ἣν ἔθου.
ΤΕΚΜΗΣΣΑ.
τί δῆτ᾽ ἂν ὡς ἐκ τῶνδ᾽ ἂν ὠφελοῖμί σε;
ΑΙΑΣ.
δός μοι προσειπεῖν αὐτὸν ἐμφανῆ τ᾽ ἰδεῖν.
ΤΕΚΜΗΣΣΑ.
καὶ μὴν πέλας γε προσπόλοις φυλάσσεται.
ΑΙΑΣ.
τί δῆτα μέλλει μὴ οὐ παρουσίαν ἔχειν; 540
ΤΕΚΜΗΣΣΑ.
ὦ παῖ, πατὴρ καλεῖ σε. δεῦρο προσπόλων
ἄγ᾽ αὐτὸν ὅσπερ χερσὶν εὐθύνων κυρεῖς.
ΑΙΑΣ.
ἕρποντι φωνεῖς, ἢ λελειμμένῳ λόγων;

537. τί δῆτ᾽ ἂν ὡς ἐκ τῶνδ᾽ ἂν ὠφελοῖμί σε; "In what after this (that is, after your approval of what I have already done) can I further benefit you?" Cf. 823, ἐκ δὲ τῶνδέ μοι, "but after this (that is, since the case with me is such as I have stated it) do you first, O Jupiter, assist me" &c. Be it observed that ἐκ τῶνδε means the same as ὡς ἐκ τῶνδε, ὡς being used only as a strengthening particle in limiting propositions or statements. Matth. Gr. Gr. 628, 3. See note on v. 395.

540. μὴ οὐ is used with an infin. after negative propositions or verbs, or after interrogative sentences, which imply a negation. Thus, "why does he delay?" (τί μέλλει,) is equivalent to "let him not delay." Cf. O. T. 565, Trach. 90, and Xen. Cyr. 2. 2. 20.

543. ἢ λελειμμένῳ λόγων; At v. 541 Tecmessa may be supposed to call aloud for the child, as if he were at a great distance off. Ajax therefore asks, "Do you call to one who attends to you, and is now approaching, or to one who is so far off that he does not hear you?" Rightly the Schol., ἐγγὺς ὄντι, ἢ ἀπολιμπανομένῳ τῆς κλήσεως, ἤγουν οὐκ ἀκούοντι—literally, "to one who falls short of your calling." Cf. Eur. Or. 1085, and Helen. 1246, λέλειμμαι τῶν ἐν Ἕλλησιν νόμων.

52   ΣΟΦΟΚΛΕΟΥΣ

ΤΕΚΜΗΣΣΑ.
καὶ δὴ κομίζει προσπόλων ὅδ᾽ ἐγγύθεν.
           ΑΙΑΣ.
αἶρ᾽ αὐτόν, αἶρε δεῦρο. ταρβήσει γὰρ οὐ   545
νεοσφαγῆ που τόνδε προσλεύσσων φόνον,
εἴπερ δικαίως ἔστ᾽ ἐμὸς τὰ πατρόθεν.
ἀλλ᾽ αὐτίκ᾽ ὠμοῖς αὐτὸν ἐν νομοῖς πατρὸς
δεῖ πωλοδαμνεῖν κἀξομοιοῦσθαι φύσιν.
ὦ παῖ, γένοιο πατρὸς εὐτυχέστερος,   550
τὰ δ᾽ ἄλλ᾽ ὅμοιος· καὶ γένοι᾽ ἂν οὐ κακός.

545—584. "This whole speech of Ajax carries with it the air and form of his Last Will and Testament. He gives orders to his wife and family, as a man immediately about to quit the world." Francklin. To these just remarks we may add, that at the close of this speech he plainly tells his friends in what way and manner he was about to quit the world. He tells them that his only remedy for his ills is his own sword. Long before this he had given expression to this thought. He wished for death. In v. 394 he beseeches Erebus to receive him into the place of darkness, as being to him more desirable than the brightest light of day; for what, says he, is there left for me in life? Afterwards addressing himself to all the well-known scenes about Troy, he takes his farewell of them, he says, no longer, no longer shall ye see me alive. Then in the following speech he sums up the whole of his speculations on human life and the objects and desires of men with the observation, that now to die honourably (that is, with his own hand) is the only thing left for him to do. Therefore neither the Chorus nor Tecmessa was left in the slightest doubt as to the self-destruction which Ajax was meditating. All that remained for them to hope was, that they might possibly turn away his thoughts from it before he had formed the fixed resolve. First the Chorus begs him to leave these thoughts and be ruled by his friends. Then in a most pathetic address, which it has often been observed is in some respects similar to the parting of Hector and Andromache in Il. 6, Tecmessa earnestly entreats him not to leave her unprotected, but to take pity on herself and his own son, and to think how great a misery he would bring on them by his voluntary death. Then she concludes with an artful turn of the conclusion of his own speech—that if he thought it became a noble-minded man to die honourably, it was no less true that it did not become a noble-minded man to retain no grateful remembrance of the kind treatment which he had received from another, such as she had shown towards him (523).

ΑΙΑΣ.

καίτοι σε καὶ νῦν τοῦτό γε ζηλοῦν ἔχω,
ὁθούνεκ' οὐδὲν τῶνδ' ἐπαισθάνει κακῶν.
ἐν τῷ φρονεῖν γὰρ μηδὲν ἥδιστος βιος,
τὸ μὴ φρονεῖν γὰρ κάρτ' ἀνώδυνον κακόν.
ἕως τὸ χαίρειν καὶ τὸ λυπεῖσθαι μάθῃς. 555
ὅταν δ' ἵκῃ πρὸς τοῦτο, δεῖ σ' ὅπως πατρὸς
δείξεις ἐν ἐχθροῖς οἷος ἐξ οἵου 'τράφης.
τέως δὲ κούφοις πνεύμασιν βόσκου, νέαν
ψυχὴν ἀτάλλων, μητρὶ τῇδε χαρμονήν.
οὔτοι σ' Ἀχαιῶν, οἶδα, μή τις ὑβρίσῃ 560
στυγναῖσι λώβαις, οὐδὲ χωρὶς ὄντ' ἐμοῦ.
τοῖον πυλωρὸν φύλακα Τεῦκρον ἀμφί σοι
λείψω τροφῆς ἄοκνον ἔμπα, κεἰ τανῦν
τηλωπὸς οἰχνεῖ, δυσμενῶν θήραν ἔχων.
ἀλλ', ἄνδρες ἀσπιστῆρες, ἐνάλιος λεώς, 565
ὑμῖν τε κοινὴν τήνδ' ἐπισκήπτω χάριν,
κείνῳ τ' ἐμὴν ἀγγείλατ' ἐντολήν, ὅπως
τὸν παῖδα τόνδε πρὸς δόμους ἐμοὺς ἄγων
Τελαμῶνι δείξει μητρί τ', Ἐρίβοιαν λέγω,
ὥς σφιν γένηται γηροβοσκὸς εἰσαεί. 570
[μέχρις οὗ μυχοὺς κίχωσι τοῦ κάτω θεοῦ.]
καὶ τἀμὰ τεύχη μήτ' ἀγωνάρχαι τινὲς
θήσουσ' Ἀχαιοῖς μήθ' ὁ λυμεὼν ἐμός.

559. χαρμονὴν is an accus. in apposition with the sentence.
571. This verse appears to be rightly rejected by Elmsley and Dindorf, not only because μέχρι and ἄχρι are foreign to tragic and even Attic usage, but because an anapaest composed of two little words does not suit the harmony which is observed in more ancient tragedy.
573. Dindorf rightly observes that μήτ'... θήσουσι depends on ὅπως in v. 567. This is not the only occasion where a full stop, as after εἰσαεὶ in v. 570, separates what ought rightly to be considered as only one complete sentence. See notes on vv. 412 foll. and 771 foll. The proper order would be, ὁ ἐμὸς λυμεών. Cf. Eur. Hipp. 683, ὁ γεννήτωρ ἐμὸς, which is quite sufficient to show that the change is admissible in Greek poetry, when the pers. pron. immediately follows, "no-

ἀλλ' αὐτό μοι σὺ, παῖ, λαβὼν ἐπώνυμον,
Εὐρύσακες, ἴσχε διὰ πολυρράφου στρέφων   575
πόρπακος ἑπτάβοιον ἄρρηκτον σάκος·
τὰ δ' ἄλλα τεύχη κοίν' ἐμοὶ τεθάψεται.
ἀλλ' ὡς τάχος τὸν παῖδα τόνδ' ἤδη δέχου,
καὶ δῶμα πάκτου, μηδ' ἐπισκήνους γόους
δάκρυε. κάρτα τοι φιλοίκτιστον γυνή.   580
πύκαζε θᾶσσον. οὐ πρὸς ἰατροῦ σοφοῦ
θρηνεῖν ἐπῳδὰς πρὸς τομῶντι πήματι.

ΧΟΡΟΣ.
δέδοικ' ἀκούων τήνδε τὴν προθυμίαν.
οὐ γάρ μ' ἀρέσκει γλῶσσά σου τεθηγμένη.

ΤΕΚΜΗΣΣΑ.
ὦ δέσποτ' Αἴας, τί ποτε δρασείεις φρενί;   585

ΑΙΑΣ.
μὴ κρῖνε, μὴ 'ξέταζε. σωφρονεῖν καλόν.

ΤΕΚΜΗΣΣΑ.
οἴμ' ὡς ἀθυμῶ· καί σε πρὸς τοῦ σοῦ τέκνου
καὶ θεῶν ἱκνοῦμαι μὴ προδοὺς ἡμᾶς γένῃ.

ΑΙΑΣ.
ἄγαν γε λυπεῖς. οὐ κάτοισθ' ἐγὼ θεοῖς
ὡς οὐδὲν ἀρκεῖν εἴμ' ὀφειλέτης ἔτι;   590

mine et pronomine tanquam in unum coalescente." Dindorf.

589. οὐ κάτοισθ' ἐγὼ θεοῖς ὡς οὐδὲν ἀρκεῖν εἴμ' ὀφειλέτης ἔτι; Nothing can show in a more striking manner the resolute purpose of Ajax to destroy himself than his brief answers to Tecmessa in this his last colloquy with her. She had just been conjuring him by the gods not to desert her. To this he replies, "Do you not know that I am now no longer a debtor to the gods to render them any duty or service?" which is as much as to say, "I am resolved to die. The gods can do me no further good or ill, and therefore I am no longer a debtor to them." Brunck quotes Aen. 11. 51, and Lobeck quotes Maximinian, Eleg. 5. 231, "Nil mihi cum Superis: explevi munera vitae." Yet the

ΤΕΚΜΗΣΣΑ.
εὔφημα φώνει.
ΑΙΑΣ.
τοῖς ἀκούουσιν λέγε.
ΤΕΚΜΗΣΣΑ.
σὺ δ' οὐχὶ πείσει;
ΑΙΑΣ.
πόλλ' ἄγαν ἤδη θροεῖς.
ΤΕΚΜΗΣΣΑ.
ταρβῶ γάρ, ὦναξ.
ΑΙΑΣ.
οὐ ξυνέρξεθ' ὡς τάχος;
ΤΕΚΜΗΣΣΑ.
πρὸς θεῶν, μαλάσσου.
ΑΙΑΣ.
μῶρά μοι δοκεῖς φρονεῖν,
εἰ τοὐμὸν ἦθος ἄρτι παιδεύειν νοεῖς. 595
ΧΟΡΟΣ.
ὦ κλεινὰ Σαλαμίς, σὺ μέν που   στρ. α΄.
ναίεις ἁλίπλακτος, εὐδαίμων,
πᾶσιν περίφαντος ἀεί·
ἐγὼ δ' ὁ τλάμων, παλαιὸς ἀφ' οὗ χρόνος, 600

sentiment as expressed by Ajax was considered by Tecmessa to be a very irreverent one, for she mildly expostulates with him, and entreats him to speak words of better omen. When she still persisted in her earnest entreaties, he showed the utmost impatience; and when again she conjures him by the gods to relent, he says,

"Thou art bereft
Of prudence, if thou form the vain design
To shake the settled purpose of my soul."—*Dale.*

600—607.
ἐγὼ δ' ὁ τλάμων, παλαιὸς ἀφ'
οὗ χρόνος,
Ἰδαίᾳ μίμνω λειμωνίᾳ ποίᾳ, μήλων
ἀνήριθμος, αἰὲν εὐνόμᾳ,
χρόνῳ τρυχόμενος,
κακὰν ἐλπίδ' ἔχων
ἔτι μέ ποτ' ἀνύσειν
τὸν ἀπότροπον ἀίδηλον Ἄιδαν.
This is substantially the reading of all the MSS. The only variations from it are Ll. μίμνῳ, Γ μίμνῶν, La. and Δ μίμνων, which are all evident mistakes. Also La. ποίαι, and Γ πόᾳ. Then

56   ΣΟΦΟΚΛΕΟΥΣ

Ἰδαίᾳ μίμνω λειμωνίᾳ ποίᾳ, μήλων
ἀνήριθμος, αἰὲν εὐνόμᾳ,

there is εὐνώμᾳ in one or two MSS., which is admitted by all to be the correction of Triclinius for the sake of metre. In consequence of the metre of v. 601 being considered to be extremely faulty, the attention of the critics has been almost entirely drawn away from the original reading of the MSS. to the various corrections of it which have been suggested, out of which that of Hermann has been generally accepted as the best, and now appears in most modern editions. The note of Mr. Jebb on the passage as amended by Hermann is a signal instance of the very scant attention which has been paid to the reading of the MSS.; for while he notices several of the conjectural emendations of it, he says nothing about the original reading itself, except so far as to inform his readers that "a variant for μηνῶν is μήλων." So far from this being the case, μήλων is the one only reading of all the MSS. and the scholia, and μηνῶν was never heard of until Hermann dreamed of it. Thenceforth μήλων, which is the key to the meaning of the whole passage, was hardly thought worthy of the slightest notice. The sentence with μήλων may be construed thus: "For I the wretched one, it is a long time dating back from an early period (of our coming hither), having the charge of a countless number of sheep, have been dwelling in the grassy meadows of Ida, that at all seasons of the year afford good pasture; I that am worn out with the length of time, and have now the miserable expectation of yet accomplishing the journey to the abhorred shades of Hades." The sentence is consistent in all its parts, and presents to us a picturesque description of a company of shepherds in Mount Ida, who had up to this time been feeding their flocks there with much contentment, but over whom now a gloom was cast, and all prospect of a happy termination of their labours was taken away by reason of a dire calamity which had befallen their mighty chief.—παλαιὸς ἀφ' οὗ χρόνος is a periphrasis for πάλαι.—εὐνόμᾳ is the Doric form for εὐνόμῳ. It is rightly joined by the Scholiast to λειμωνίᾳ ποίᾳ, and rightly interpreted by him εὐνόμᾳ λειμῶνι, τῷ καλὰς νομὰς ἔχοντι. With respect to μήλων ἀνήριθμος, it is a peculiar phrase. Its peculiarity consists in the transference of the numeral adjective from the things which are countless to the person who is the owner of them. Fortunately the same phrase is found in other places in Sophocles, or perhaps we should never have come to know its meaning here. O. T. 179, ὧν (sc. νεκρῶν) πόλις ἀνήριθμος. El. 232, θρήνων ἀνήριθμος. Trach. 247, χρόνον ... ἡμερῶν ἀνήριθμον. Thus in O. T. 179 the city itself is said to be uncounted in the number of its dead bodies that lay unburied in the plain. In El. 232 the mourner herself was uncounted in the number of her lamentations, and in Trach. 247 the time was uncounted in the number of its days. So here in

ΑΙΑΣ. 57

χρόνῳ τρυχόμενος, 605
κακὰν ἐλπίδ' ἔχων
ἔτι μέ ποτ' ἀνύσειν
τὸν ἀπότροπον ἀΐδηλον Ἀιδαν.
καί μοι δυσθεράπευτος Αἴας ἀντ. α'.
ξύνεστιν ἔφεδρος, ὤμοι μοι, 610
θείᾳ μανίᾳ ξύναυλος·
ὃν ἐξεπέμψω πρὶν δή ποτε θουρίῳ

Aj. 602 the leader of the Chorus, instead of saying that the sheep were countless, spoke of himself and his associates as being countless in the number of their sheep. Thus it appears that the Chorus had been for a long time keepers of large flocks of sheep and other cattle in the ever-green valleys of Mount Ida, and this fact fully explains the reason why in v. 360 Ajax addressed them as a company of shepherds. The two passages throw light on each other, and the accidental and undesigned coincidence between them goes a great way to prove the genuineness of the text in both places. I call it a perfectly undesigned coincidence; for we cannot for a moment suppose that the poet wrote ποιμένων in v. 360, because he intended to explain it in v. 602. Most probably no explanation was required; for as it has always been usual for actors to personate the characters they were intended to represent, so in all probability the Chorus appeared on the stage habited as shepherds, so as to be known and recognized at once as such by all the spectators. Otherwise an Athenian assembly of spectators would have been quite as much embarrassed at hearing the Chorus addressed as shepherds, as the mere readers of the play have been since. But it may be said that all this is inconsistent with what the Chorus says in vv. 1185—1223 concerning the miseries of war. This objection will be met in the note on that passage. The main objection, however, has always been considered to be the metre. This note has been so long, and the question of metre requires such careful attention, that it is left to be discussed and examined in the Appendix.

609—611. καί μοι . . . ξύναυλος. With respect to the word ἔφεδρος, may it not mean "sitting heavily upon me"? "And as for me, the incurable Ajax is with me, pressing heavily on my mind." Cf. Aesch. 637, βαρὺς δ' ἐφίζει, where the divine avenger of wrong is said to sit heavily on the house of him who had done the wrong. In the present case the sad condition of Ajax sits as an incubus on the mind of the Chorus, and is felt by him to be a heavy calamity to himself and his associates—φίλοις μέγα πένθος εὕρηται. It is usually construed, "and besides the incurable Ajax is present with me a fresh antagonist." This appears to be too technical a sense to suit the passage.

58   ΣΟΦΟΚΛΕΟΥΣ

κρατοῦντ᾽ ἐν Ἄρει· νῦν δ᾽ αὖ φρενὸς οἰοβότης
φίλοις μέγα πένθος ηὕρηται.   615
τὰ πρὶν δ᾽ ἔργα χεροῖν
μεγίστας ἀρετᾶς
ἄφιλα παρ᾽ ἀφίλοις   620
ἔπεσ᾽ ἔπεσε μελέοις Ἀτρείδαις.
ἦ που παλαιᾷ μὲν ἔντροφος ἁμέρᾳ,   στρ. β΄. 622
λευκῷ δὲ γήρᾳ μάτηρ νιν ὅταν νοσοῦντα   625
φρενομόρως ἀκούσῃ,
αἴλινον αἴλινον

614. φρενὸς οἰοβότης. In its primary sense the word οἰοβότης seems to mean "one of the herd that wanders away from the rest and *feeds alone*." Hence the poet, dropping the idea of feeding, applies the expression in combination with φρενὸς to one who wanders from his right mind. Schol. οὐ σὺν φρεσὶν, ἀλλ᾽ ἐκτὸς φρενῶν διάγων· ἢ ἀποπλανηθεὶς, ἀπὸ μεταφορᾶς τῶν πλανηθέντων προβάτων, καὶ μόνων βοσκομένων. The word οἰοβότης is opposed to συμβότης and συμβόσκομαι. In Sept. Isa. 11. 6 this latter word is used without any reference whatever to the nature of the food which is fed upon, but simply to express the idea of consorting together in amity. φρενὸς οἰοβ. is thought to mean "feeding on his mind," but οἶος rather refers to the object from which he feeds apart, than the kind of food which is fed upon.

616. τὰ πρὶν δ᾽ ἔργα χεροῖν. "His former deeds of noblest valour have fallen, have fallen away unvalued, receiving no return of love from the loveless and miserable Atridae." — μελέοις, *wretched* or *miserable*, is used as a term of reproach in the sense of *vile* or *despicable*.

622—634. ἦ που παλαιᾷ... ἄμυγμα χαίτας. "No doubt his aged and unhappy mother, when she hears of his mental malady, will pour forth not indeed the low mourning strain, Ah! Linos, Linos, nor yet the plaintive note of that piteous bird the nightingale, but shrill piercing cries will she wail out, with beatings of her breast and rendings of her hoary locks." Those critics who follow the Scholiast and think that οὐδὲ has the force of a double negative are, I believe, right. Cf. Thuc. 8. 99, where see Arnold's note on the words αἱ Φοίνισσαι νῆες οὐδὲ ὁ Τισσαφέρνης. Also cf. Lucian. Verae Historiae, I. 655, ἔντερον δὲ ἐν αὐτῇ, οὐδὲ ἧπαρ φαίνεται, and 2. 682, δένδρον δὲ οὐδὲ ὕδωρ ἐνῆν. The word αἴλινον is supposed to have meant a lamentation for the death of Linos. The conjecture calls to mind a lamentation which appears to have been annually observed by the Tyrians, and which is so finely described in Milton, Par. Lost, I. 446.

ΑΙΑΣ.

οὐδ' οἰκτρᾶς γόον ὄρνιθος ἀηδοῦς
ἤσει δύσμορος, ἀλλ' ὀξυτόνους μὲν ᾠδὰς   630
θρηνήσει, χερόπληκτοι δ'
ἐν στέρνοισι πεσοῦνται
δοῦποι καὶ πολιᾶς ἄμυγμα χαίτας.
κρείσσων γὰρ "Αιδᾳ κεύθων ἢ νοσῶν μάταν,   ἀντ. β'.
ὃς ἐκ πατρῴας ἥκων γενεᾶς ἄριστος   636
πολυπόνων Ἀχαιῶν,
οὐκ ἔτι συντρόφοις
ὀργαῖς ἔμπεδος, ἀλλ' ἐκτὸς ὁμιλεῖ.   640
ὦ τλᾶμον πάτερ, οἵαν σε μένει πυθέσθαι
παιδὸς δύσφορον ἄταν,
ἃν οὔπω τις ἔθρεψεν
αἰὼν Αἰακιδᾶν ἄτερθε τοῦδε.   645

ΑΙΑΣ.

ἅπανθ' ὁ μακρὸς κἀναρίθμητος χρόνος
φύει τ' ἄδηλα καὶ φανέντα κρύπτεται·
κοὐκ ἔστ' ἄελπτον οὐδὲν, ἀλλ' ἁλίσκεται
χὠ δεινὸς ὅρκος χαἰ περισκελεῖς φρένες.
κἀγὼ γὰρ, ὃς τὰ δείν' ἐκαρτέρουν τότε,   650
βαφῇ σίδηρος ὣς ἐθηλύνθην στόμα

635. κρείσσων γὰρ "Αιδᾳ κεύθων ἢ νοσῶν μάταν. By the disjunctive ἢ the two states, "Αιδᾳ κεύθων and νοσῶν μάταν, are put into opposition to each other. So in O. T. 1368, κρείσσων γὰρ ἦσθα μηκέτ' ὢν ἢ ζῶν τυφλὸς, and in Lys. 26. 4, κρείττων ἦν ὁ πατήρ σου μὴ λειτουργήσας ἢ τοσαῦτα τῶν ἑαυτοῦ ἀναλώσας. This is in accordance with the style of all Greek writers, while the correction ὁ νοσῶν is not in the style of any of them. The reason for the correction is discussed in the Appendix on note

600—608. It is to be observed that the Chorus now some time after Ajax had recovered from his senseless madness, speaks of him here as being still so badly diseased in his mind that death was better to him than life, and that throughout the foregoing part of this lamentation his present diseased state of mind is expressed in the strongest terms.

651. βαφῇ σίδηρος ὥς. Whatever might have been the process by which iron was rendered soft and malleable, it is enough to know that there was such a pro-

ΣΟΦΟΚΛΕΟΤΣ

πρὸς τῆσδε τῆς γυναικός· οἰκτείρω δέ νιν
χήραν παρ' ἐχθροῖς παῖδά τ' ὀρφανὸν λιπεῖν.
ἀλλ' εἶμι πρός τε λουτρὰ καὶ παρακτίους
λειμῶνας, ὡς ἂν λύμαθ' ἁγνίσας ἐμὰ 655
μῆνιν βαρεῖαν ἐξαλεύσωμαι θεᾶς·
μολών τε χῶρον ἔνθ' ἂν ἀστιβῆ κίχω
κρύψω τόδ' ἔγχος τοὐμόν, ἔχθιστον βελῶν,
γαίας ὀρύξας ἔνθα μή τις ὄψεται·
ἀλλ' αὐτὸ νὺξ Ἅιδης τε σωζόντων κάτω. 660
ἐγὼ γὰρ ἐξ οὗ χειρὶ τοῦτ' ἐδεξάμην
παρ' Ἕκτορος δώρημα δυσμενεστάτου,
οὔπω τι κεδνὸν ἔσχον Ἀργείων πάρα.

cess, and that fact is evidenced by the use of the same simile in the following passages adduced by Lobeck: Plat. Rep. 3. 411 B, εἴ τι θυμοειδὲς εἶχεν, ὥσπερ σίδηρον ἐμάλαξε καὶ χρήσιμον ἐξ ἀχρήστου ἐποίησεν. Plutarch. Vitae Num. c. 8, τὴν πόλιν καθάπερ σίδηρον ἐκ σκληρᾶς μαλακωτέραν ποιῆσαι.

656. μῆνιν βαρεῖαν ἐξαλεύσωμαι θεᾶς. "That I may avert from myself the heavy anger of the goddess," that is, of Athene. La., Ll., and other MSS. ἐξαλεύσωμαι. Hesychius has ἐξαλύξωμαι, which is preferred by Dindorf. Hes. Opp. 105, 756, 800, ἐξαλέασθαι. In Il. 5. 34, and again in 16. 711, we find the Mid. v. ἀλεύομαι used with respect to the avoiding of the wrath of a god, as it is here. "Restitui ἐξαλεύσωμαι ob codd. plurimorum consensum, et ut usitatius. Futuro ἀλύξομαι usus est Hesiodus Opp. 363. Aoristum non reperio." Lobeck.

659. γαίας ὀρύξας ἔνθα μή τις ὄψεται. Here γαίας becomes a partitive genitive in consequence of its being governed by ἔνθα, which is partitive in its signification, as all local adverbs are. V. 387, οὐχ ὁρᾷς ἵν' εἶ κακοῦ, "into what a depth of misery you are fallen." Be it observed, however, that ἔνθα being here used as a relative, in the sense of where or in what part of a place, its proper position is rather after the genitive than before it, namely, at the head of the clause which follows and depends upon it. Cf. Hdt. 2. 172, ἵδρυσε τῆς πόλιος ὅκου ἦν ἐπιτηδεώτατον. Phil. 1181, ἴωμεν ναὸς ἵν' ἡμῖν τέτακται. We may construe it, "having dug in a part of the earth where no one shall see it."—ἔνθα μή τις ὄψεται. The indic. future, in what is called the recta oratio, seems to be used, when required after μή, as freely as the indic. pres., and more particularly in relative clauses. Thus in O. T. 569, ἐφ' οἷς γὰρ μὴ φρονῶ σιγᾶν φιλῶ; but in 1412, ἐκρίψατ' ἔνθα μήποτ' εἰσόψεθ' ἔτι. Also Trach. 799, El. 380, O. C. 1186, and An. 691.

ΑΙΑΣ.

ἀλλ' ἔστ' ἀληθὴς ἡ βροτῶν παροιμια,
ἐχθρῶν ἄδωρα δῶρα κοὐκ ὀνήσιμα.   665
τοιγὰρ τὸ λοιπὸν εἰσόμεσθα μὲν θεοῖς
εἴκειν, μαθησόμεσθα δ' Ἀτρείδας σέβειν.
ἄρχοντές εἰσιν, ὥσθ' ὑπεικτέον. τί μή;
καὶ γὰρ τὰ δεινὰ καὶ τὰ καρτερώτατα
τιμαῖς ὑπείκει· τοῦτο μὲν νιφοστιβεῖς   670
χειμῶνες ἐκχωροῦσιν εὐκάρπῳ θέρει·
ἐξίσταται δὲ νυκτὸς αἰανὴς κύκλος
τῇ λευκοπώλῳ φέγγος ἡμέρᾳ φλέγειν·
δεινῶν τ' ἄημα πνευμάτων ἐκοίμισε
στένοντα πόντον· ἐν δ' ὁ παγκρατὴς ὕπνος   675
λύει πεδήσας, οὐδ' ἀεὶ λαβὼν ἔχει.
ἡμεῖς δὲ πῶς οὐ γνωσόμεσθα σωφρονεῖν;
ἐγὼ δ', ἐπίσταμαι γὰρ ἀρτίως ὅτι

665. The proverbial sentence, "the gifts of enemies are giftless and profitless," is expressed, though in a less striking way, in Eur. Med. 618, κακοῦ γὰρ ἀνδρὸς δῶρ' ὄνησιν οὐκ ἔχει.

672. νυκτὸς αἰανὴς κύκλος. This is usually construed, "the vault of gloomy night," but the expression, *the vault of night*, is as unusual and peculiar as its opposite would be, *the vault of day*. On the other hand, if it be construed, as it may be quite literally, "the orb of gloomy night," what other orb could it signify but that of the moon?—κύκλος is frequently used in the three tragic poets for the sun's bright orb, and sometimes, as in Eur. Iph. Aul. 717 and Ion 115, for the orb of the moon. Cf. Eur. Iph. Taur. 110, νυκτὸς ὄμμα λυγαίας, which is much the same as νυκτὸς αἰανὴς ὄμμα. Ellendt in his Lex. Soph., after giving his assent to the usual way of construing v. 672, yet ends with saying, "Fateor tamen valde blandiri νυκτὸς αἰανὴς κύκλος, ut luna significetur soli cedens."

674. Cf. Hor. I. 3. 15.—ἐν δ'. Cf. O. C. 55, O. T. 181, An. 420, and Trach. 206. "Simul aut inter haec, sive etiam significare videtur." Wunder.

678. ἐγὼ δ', ἐπίσταμαι γάρ. ἐγὼ δ' is elliptical. The speaker had just before said, "How shall we not learn moderation?" He then gives answer to himself, "but I"—(that is, but I *have learned it*,) for I am now aware" &c. Cf. Plat. Laches. 200 c, νῦν δὲ, ὁμοίως γὰρ πάντες ἐν ἀπορίᾳ ἐγενόμεθα. The speaker had just before said, that if he had appeared to know better than the rest of the company how to educate certain youths, it would

ΣΟΦΟΚΛΕΟΥΣ

ὅ τ' ἐχθρὸς ἡμῖν ἐς τοσόνδ' ἐχθαρτέος,
ὡς καὶ φιλήσων αὖθις, ἔς τε τὸν φίλον   680
τοσαῦθ' ὑπουργῶν ὠφελεῖν βουλήσομαι,
ὡς αἰὲν οὐ μενοῦντα. τοῖς πολλοῖσι γὰρ
βροτῶν ἄπιστός ἐσθ' ἑταιρείας λιμήν.
ἀλλ' ἀμφὶ μὲν τούτοισιν εὖ σχήσει· σὺ δὲ
ἔσω θεοῖς ἐλθοῦσα διὰ τέλους, γύναι,   685
εὔχου τελεῖσθαι τοὐμὸν ὧν ἐρᾷ κέαρ.
ὑμεῖς θ' ἑταῖροι ταυτὰ τῇδέ μοι τάδε
τιμᾶτε, Τεύκρῳ τ', ἢν μόλῃ, σημήνατε
μέλειν μὲν ἡμῶν, εὐνοεῖν δ' ὑμῖν ἅμα.
ἐγὼ γὰρ εἶμ' ἐκεῖσ' ὅποι πορευτέον·   690
ὑμεῖς δ' ἃ φράζω δρᾶτε, καὶ τάχ' ἄν μ' ἴσως
πύθοισθε, κεἰ νῦν δυστυχῶ, σεσωσμένον.

be proper for him to undertake that work; "but now (*this is not the case*,) for (in our previous discussions upon the subject) we were all in a similar state of doubt." This is quite in accordance with the idiom of the Greek language.

680. ἔς τε τὸν φίλον. The construction is, ἔς τε τὸν φίλον τοσαῦτα ὑπουργῶν, ὡς (ἐς τὸν) αἰὲν οὐ μενοῦντα, ὠφελεῖν (αὐτὸν) βουλήσομαι.—ὠφελεῖν is a verb which seems always to have for its object a person, seldom or never an inanimate thing, or abstract notion or feeling. For this cause I consider that the usual way of construing O. C. 436, οὐδεὶς ἔρωτος τοῦδ' ἐφαίνετ' ὠφελῶν, is indefensible, and that the right way is, "by reason of this desire of mine, (or) on account of this desire of mine, no one came forward to assist me in it." ἔρωτος τοῦδε is the genitive of the cause, as τοῦ δὲ σοῦ ψόφου is in Aj. 1116.

684. ἀλλ' ἀμφὶ μὲν τούτοισιν εὖ σχήσει. "But about this matter (that is, about submitting to my rulers) all will be right with me." All that he meant was, that he would cease henceforth from any further contention with them, by destroying himself.

691. καὶ τάχ' ἄν μ' ἴσως.

"And soon perchance, though
 now in misery sunk,
My glad release from sorrow
 shall ye hear."—*Dale*.

The whole of this speech is ironical. A studied ambiguity pervades it—where Ajax wishes his friends to understand that he will soon be restored to a perfect state of health and prosperity, whereas his real meaning is that he is about to end all his miseries in death.

ΑΙΑΣ.

ΧΟΡΟΣ.

ἔφριξ᾽ ἔρωτι, περιχαρὴς δ᾽ ἀνεπτόμαν. στρ.
ἰὼ ἰὼ Πὰν Πάν,
ὢ Πὰν Πὰν ἁλίπλαγκτε, Κυλλανίας χιονοκτύπου

693—717. "I thrill with love, and spring up with joy. O Pan, Pan, O sea-roaming Pan, thou leader of the choir of the gods, show thyself from the rocky ridge of snow-covered Cyllene, and take part with us in the self-taught Nysian Gnossian dances: for now it is my wish to join the choir of dancers; and thou Apollo, Delian king, hastening over the Icarian waves, and making thy presence easily discernible, be with us ever propitious. Ares has removed a dark cloud of grief from our eyes. O Zeus, now again a bright day pours its beams of gladness on our ships, since Ajax has forgotten his troubles, and reverently offers sacrifice to the gods, worshipping them with a due observance of all accustomed rites. Great Time withers all things ... and I should say that nothing was impossible, since even Ajax has repented of his (seemingly) desperate wrath and strifes with the Atridae." In this translation it is assumed, in conformity with the opinion of the great majority of critics and editors, that the words τε καὶ φλέγει, which follow μαραίνει, are by the evidence of metre the addition or interpolation of some grammarian, who thus thought that the observation upon Time would be more complete. These three words have certainly nothing to answer them in the corr. v. 701 of the strophe; but is it not just as probable that v. 701 may have lost something out of it, which answered to τε καὶ φλέγει, as that these words have been improperly added to v. 714? With respect to the sense of the passage, it should not be lost sight of that this whole song of the Chorus is one of unbounded joy after a period of deep depression; but μαραίνει standing alone presents to us no other idea than one which is allied to sorrow and sadness; for it signifies, to cause to die away, to waste away, to fade and to decay; whereas if the words τε καὶ φλέγει be suffered to remain, the case is reversed, and the sense is, "Great Time, which withers all things, *and again kindles them into brightness*, has now caused a bright day to dawn on us, who were before in the deepest gloom, by the recovery of Ajax from what seemed to us a desperate state of insanity." Without those words the observation upon Time is one-sided. It views Time only as destroying all things, but not at all as quickening into new life that which seemed to have been destroyed. In v. 717 the MSS. vary between θυμὸν, θυμόν τ᾽, and θυμῶν. The conj. emend. θυμοῦ is now generally accepted. The above translation assumes that θυμῶν is the right reading, and that ἀέλπτων taken as an adjective agrees with it and with νεικέων.

695. ἁλίπλαγκτε. Whatever may have been the cause of this epithet being applied to Pan, the character of a sea-roaming god

64 ΣΟΦΟΚΛΕΟΥΣ

πετραίας ἀπὸ δειράδος φάνηθ', ὦ 696
θεῶν χοροποί' ἄναξ, ὅπως μοι
Νύσια Κνώσι' ὀρχήματ' αὐτοδαῆ ξυνὼν ἰάψῃς. 700
νῦν γὰρ ἐμοὶ μέλει χορεῦσαι.
Ἰκαρίων δ' ὑπὲρ πελαγέων μολὼν ἄναξ Ἀπόλλων
ὁ Δάλιος, εὔγνωστος
ἐμοὶ ξυνείης διὰ παντὸς εὔφρων. 705
ἔλυσεν αἰνὸν ἄχος ἀπ' ὀμμάτων Ἄρης. ἀντ.
ἰὼ ἰώ. νῦν αὖ,
νῦν, ὦ Ζεῦ, πάρα λευκὸν εὐάμερον πελάσαι φάος
θοᾶν ὠκυάλων νεῶν, ὅτ' Αἴας 710
λαθίπονος πάλιν, θεῶν δ' αὖ
πάνθυτα θέσμι' ἐξήνυσ' εὐνομίᾳ σέβων μεγίστᾳ.
πάνθ' ὁ μέγας χρόνος μαραίνει,
κοὐδὲν ἀναύδατον φατίσαιμ' ἄν, εὗτέ γ' ἐξ ἀέλπτων
Αἴας μετανεγνώσθη 716

is clearly ascribed to him in a line of Nonnus, 43. 214, ἀβάτοισιν ἐφ' ὕδασι κοῦφος ὁδίτης. It is the more applicable to him on the present occasion, because he is invoked by the Choir to come to them from Mount Cyllene in Arcadia, which was on the other side of the Aegean Sea. "Tu qui maria pervagari soles, adesdum mare Aegaeum transvectus." Lobeck.

700. The Nysian Gnossian dances, which took their names from Nysa the birthplace of Dionysus, and Gnossus in Crete, appear to have been of a wild and rude character, unrestrained within any rules of art, and hence they are called αὐτοδαῆ.

706. ἔλυσεν αἰνὸν ἄχος...Ἄρης. The god of strife is here specially spoken of as having removed a bitter grief simply by ceasing to stir up that strife which had occasioned it, in the same manner as in vv. 675, 676 all-powerful sleep is said to loose its subjects from its power simply by ceasing to exert its power over them, and the blast of the mighty winds is said to lull the ocean to rest simply by ceasing to disturb it.

709. νῦν αὖ, νῦν, ὦ Ζεῦ, πάρα λευκὸν κ.τ.λ. The order of the words as to their construction is, πάρεστι λευκὸν εὐάμερον φάος, (ὥστε) πελάσαι νεῶν.

712. πάνθ. θέσμια, "all the sacrificial ordinances of the gods." —εὐν. σέβ. μ., "worshipping them in strictest conformity with the prescribed ritual."—ἐξήνυσ', "has fully performed."

715. κοὐδὲν ἀναύδατον, "nothing that might not be spoken of as a possible fact," and so nothing that was not possible.

716. μετανεγνώσθη, "has come to another mind." With respect

ΑΙΑΣ.

θυμοῦ τ' Ἀτρείδαις μεγάλων τε νεικέων.

ΑΓΓΕΛΟΣ.

ἄνδρες φίλοι, τὸ πρῶτον ἀγγεῖλαι θέλω,
Τεῦκρος πάρεστιν ἄρτι Μυσίων ἀπὸ   720
κρημνῶν· μέσον δὲ προσμολὼν στρατήγιον
κυδάζεται τοῖς πᾶσιν Ἀργείοις ὁμοῦ.
στείχοντα γὰρ πρόσωθεν αὐτὸν ἐν κύκλῳ
μαθόντες ἀμφέστησαν, εἶτ' ὀνείδεσιν
ἤρασσον ἔνθεν κἄνθεν οὔτις ἔσθ' ὃς οὔ,   725
τὸν τοῦ μανέντος κἀπιβουλευτοῦ στρατοῦ
ξύναιμον ἀποκαλοῦντες, ὡς οὐκ ἀρκέσοι
τὸ μὴ οὐ πέτροισι πᾶς καταξανθεὶς θανεῖν.
ὥστ' ἐς τοσοῦτον ἦλθον ὥστε καὶ χεροῖν
κολεῶν ἐρυστὰ διεπεραιώθη ξίφη.   730

to this word, the passage may be more literally rendered, "has come out of his wrath and strife with the Atridae to a better state of mind."

723. στείχοντα γὰρ κ.τ.λ. μαθόντες must, I think, be taken with αὐτὸν στείχοντα, in the same manner as in Hdt. 6. 100, the words Ἐρετριέες δὲ, πυνθανόμενοι τὴν στρατιὴν τὴν Περσικὴν ἐπὶ σφέας ἐπιπλέουσαν, are taken together, in the sense of: "the Eretrians hearing that a Persian armament *was sailing* against them, they entreated the Athenians to assist them," that is to say, they took advantage of the information whilst the fleet was still sailing towards them. So here, the Argives having learned that Teucer *was coming* from afar, were prepared for his approach, and as soon as he came, they stood around him in a circle.

726. τὸν ξύναιμον ... ἀπο-καλοῦντες. "Terming him *the kinsman of the maniac*—τὸν being used, because the actual words of the Greeks were ὁ τοῦ μανέντος ξύναιμος." Jebb. See note on v. 143.

727. ὡς οὐκ ἀρκέσοι. This depends on λέγοντες, which is implied in the words ὀνείδεσιν ἤρασσον, "they assailed him with reproaches ... saying that he should not ward it off, so as not to die all mangled with stones," or "that he should not save himself from being utterly crushed to death with stones." Linwood construes it, "dicentes sc. eum non prohibiturum, quin." The participle καταξανθεὶς is in the nominative, because the subject of it is the same with that of the verb ἀρκέσοι. See note on 1316.

730. διεπεραιώθη. The meaning of this may be, "so that their swords plucked from their sheaths *were passed across*," that is, from

66 ΣΟΦΟΚΛΕΟΥΣ

λήγει δ' ἔρις δραμοῦσα τοῦ προσωτάτω
ἀνδρῶν γερόντων ἐν ξυναλλαγῇ λόγου.
ἀλλ' ἡμὶν Αἴας ποῦ 'στιν, ὡς φράσω τάδε;
τοῖς κυρίοις γὰρ πάντα χρὴ δηλοῦν λόγον.

ΧΟΡΟΣ.
οὐκ ἔνδον, ἀλλὰ φροῦδος ἀρτίως, νέας 735
βουλὰς νέοισιν ἐγκαταζεύξας τρόποις.

ΑΓΓΕΛΟΣ.
ἰοὺ ἰού.
βραδεῖαν ἡμᾶς ἆρ' ὁ τήνδε τὴν ὁδὸν
πέμπων ἔπεμψεν, ἢ 'φάνην ἐγὼ βραδύς.

ΧΟΡΟΣ.
τί δ' ἐστὶ χρείας τῆσδ' ὑπεσπανισμένον; 740

ΑΓΓΕΛΟΣ.
τὸν ἄνδρ' ἀπηύδα Τεῦκρος ἔνδοθεν στέγης
μὴ 'ξω παρήκειν, πρὶν παρὼν αὐτὸς τύχοι.

ΧΟΡΟΣ.
ἀλλ' οἴχεταί τοι, πρὸς τὸ κέρδιστον τραπεὶς
γνώμης, θεοῖσιν ὡς καταλλαχθῇ χόλου.

ΑΓΓΕΛΟΣ.
ταῦτ' ἐστὶ τἄπη μωρίας πολλῆς πλέα, 745
εἴπερ τι Κάλχας εὖ φρονῶν μαντεύεται.

the left side of their persons to the right, ready for instant use.
731. δραμοῦσα τοῦ προσωτάτω. Jebb's explanation of the genitive is hardly satisfactory: "having run *somewhat* to the furthest;" for it weakens an expression which is evidently intended to be a very strong one. Lobeck compares it with Xen. An. 1. 3. 1, ἰέναι τοῦ πρόσω. Arr. Alex. 2. 6. 7, προϊέναι τοῦ πρόσω, and Philos. Ap. 1223, ἀπῆγεν αὐτὸν τοῦ πρόσω. If in these places τοῦ πρόσω means a going forwards, then τοῦ προσωτάτω must mean a going to the furthest, as it is usually explained—εἰς τὸ ἔσχατον ἐλθοῦσα Wunder; "cum longissime processisset," Musgr.

732. ἐν ξυναλλαγῇ λόγου, "through the interchange of a word;" that is, the strife when it had gone to its height was calmed down by the interposition of the elders and their wise advice. Cf. Eur. Supp. 602, λόγων ξυναλλαγαῖς.

ΑΙΑΣ. 67

ΧΟΡΟΣ.
ποῖον; τί δ' εἰδὼς τοῦδε πράγματος πέρι;
ΑΓΓΕΛΟΣ.
τοσοῦτον οἶδα καὶ παρὼν ἐτύγχανον.
ἐκ γὰρ ξυνέδρου καὶ τυραννικοῦ κύκλου
Κάλχας μεταστὰς οἶος Ἀτρειδῶν δίχα, 750
ἐς χεῖρα Τεύκρου δεξιὰν φιλοφρόνως
θεὶς εἶπε κἀπέσκηψε παντοίᾳ τέχνῃ
εἶρξαι κατ' ἦμαρ τοὐμφανὲς τὸ νῦν τόδε
Αἴανθ' ὑπὸ σκηναῖσι μηδ' ἀφέντ' ἐᾶν,
εἰ ζῶντ' ἐκεῖνον εἰσιδεῖν θέλοι ποτέ. 755
ἐλᾷ γὰρ αὐτὸν τῇδε θἠμέρᾳ μόνῃ
δίας Ἀθάνας μῆνις, ὡς ἔφη λέγων.
τὰ γὰρ περισσὰ κἀνόνητα σώματα
πίπτειν βαρείαις πρὸς θεῶν δυσπραξίαις
ἔφασχ' ὁ μάντις, ὅστις ἀνθρώπου φύσιν 760
βλαστὼν ἔπειτα μὴ κατ' ἄνθρωπον φρονῇ.
κεῖνος δ' ἀπ' οἴκων εὐθὺς ἐξορμώμενος
ἄνους καλῶς λέγοντος ηὑρέθη πατρός.
ὁ μὲν γὰρ αὐτὸν ἐννέπει, τέκνον, δόρει
βούλου κρατεῖν μέν, σὺν θεῷ δ' ἀεὶ κρατεῖν. 765
ὁ δ' ὑψικόμπως κἀφρόνως ἠμείψατο,
πάτερ, θεοῖς μὲν κἂν ὁ μηδὲν ὢν ὁμοῦ

758. τὰ γὰρ περισσὰ κἀνόνητα σώματα. "For the prophet said that overbearing and worthless persons, who having been born with only the nature of a man, yet cherish thoughts not becoming a man, do fall into sore calamities from the anger of the gods."—ἀνόνητα, literally, "useless" or "profitless." Such persons are said to incur the anger of the gods, and to be cast away as a worthless and mischievous encumbrance.—ὅστις refers sometimes to an antecedent in the plural, and may then be construed "whosoever of them," or as εἴ τις, "if any of them." Cf. El. 1505, and Xen. Cyr. 5. 5. 15.—ἔπειτα, "yet after that," is sometimes used to emphasize what follows it, as being not such a sequence as could have been reasonably expected to follow the previous state of things. Cf. Xen. Cyr. 5. 5. 12.

F 2

ΣΟΦΟΚΛΕΟΤΣ

κράτος κατακτήσαιτ'· ἐγὼ δὲ καὶ δίχα
κείνων πέποιθα τοῦτ' ἐπισπάσειν κλέος.
τοσόνδ' ἐκόμπει μῦθον. εἶτα δεύτερον   770
δίας Ἀθάνας, ἡνίκ' ὀτρύνουσά νιν
ηὐδᾶτ' ἐπ' ἐχθροῖς χεῖρα φοινίαν τρέπειν,
τότ' ἀντιφωνεῖ δεινὸν ἄρρητόν τ' ἔπος·
ἄνασσα, τοῖς ἄλλοισιν Ἀργείων πέλας
ἴστω, καθ' ἡμᾶς δ' οὔποτ' ἐκρήξει μάχη.   775
τοιοῖσδε τοῖς λόγοισιν ἀστεργῆ θεᾶς
ἐκτήσατ' ὀργήν, οὐ κατ' ἄνθρωπον φρονῶν.
ἀλλ' εἴπερ ἔστι τῇδε θἠμέρᾳ, τάχ' ἂν

771. δίας Ἀθάνας. The whole passage which begins with this genitive, and ends with φρονῶν in v. 777, seems to form but one complete sentence. Thus the genitive depends on ὀργήν. It is evident from what went before in vv. 756, 757 that the subject of δίας Ἀθάνας μῆνις is resumed here, by way of explaining the cause of the wrath of Athene. This is done in a long parenthesis. The English construction does not admit of such a long parenthesis intervening between the genitive and its noun, and we can only explain it in an English translation, by an abbreviation of the parenthesis, in some such way as follows: "then again of the goddess the divine Athene (when he replied to her exhortations with the proud word, 'I need none of your aid'), by such an impious reply he brought on himself the wrath implacable." With respect to the full stop being put after μάχη, as it usually is, see note on v. 573. In translating the whole sentence, we may begin with construing it thus: "then again with respect to the divine Athene" &c.

775. καθ' ἡμᾶς. This is frequently construed "with us," or "where I am stationed," a meaning which, as Mr. Jebb observes, is scarcely satisfactory. It sometimes occurs as a military term in Xen. Cyr. in the sense of *opposite to*, or *in front of us*, as in 6. 3. 12, προσελαύνουσι καὶ μέντοι κατ' αὐτοὺς ἡμᾶς. 7. 1. 22, and 7. 1. 24, καὶ οὕτω προσῄεσαν τρεῖς φάλαγγες ἐπὶ τὸ Κύρου στράτευμα· ἡ μὲν μία, κατὰ πρόσωπον τὸ δὲ δύο, ἡ μὲν κατὰ τὸ δεξιὸν, ἡ δὲ κατὰ τὸ εὐώνυμον. We may therefore construe the sentence, "the battle will never burst forth over against us." The idea of bursting forth implies a restraining barrier which must first be overcome. What Ajax said is, "The battle will never be such in our front as that we shall not be able to keep it in check with our own unaided strength. We shall present such a strong opposing barrier to it as will effectually prevent any violent bursting forth of it."

ΑΙΑΣ.

γενοίμεθ αὐτοῦ σὺν θεῷ σωτήριοι.
τοσαῦθ᾽ ὁ μάντις εἶφ᾽· ὁ δ᾽ εὐθὺς ἐξ ἕδρας   780
πέμπει με σοὶ φέροντα τάσδ᾽ ἐπιστολὰς
Τεῦκρος φυλάσσειν. εἰ δ᾽ ἀπεστερήμεθα,
οὐκ ἔστιν ἀνὴρ κεῖνος, εἰ Κάλχας σοφός.

ΧΟΡΟΣ.

ὦ δαΐα Τέκμησσα, δύσμορον γένος,
ὅρα μολοῦσα τόνδ᾽ ὁποῖ᾽ ἔπη θροεῖ.   785
ξυρεῖ γὰρ ἐν χρῷ τοῦτο μὴ χαίρειν τινά.

ΤΕΚΜΗΣΣΑ.

τί μ᾽ αὖ τάλαιναν, ἀρτίως πεπαυμένην
κακῶν ἀτρύτων, ἐξ ἕδρας ἀνίστατε;

ΧΟΡΟΣ.

τοῦδ᾽ εἰσάκουε τἀνδρὸς, ὡς ἥκει φέρων
Αἴαντος ἡμῖν πρᾶξιν ἣν ἤλγησ᾽ ἐγώ.   790

ΤΕΚΜΗΣΣΑ.

οἴμοι, τί φῂς, ὤνθρωπε; μῶν ὀλώλαμεν;

ΑΓΓΕΛΟΣ.

οὐκ οἶδα τὴν σὴν πρᾶξιν, Αἴαντος δ᾽ ὅτι,
θυραῖος εἴπερ ἐστὶν, οὐ θαρσῶ πέρι.

ΤΕΚΜΗΣΣΑ.

καὶ μὴν θυραῖος, ὥστε μ᾽ ὠδίνειν τί φῄς.

ΑΓΓΕΛΟΣ.

ἐκεῖνον εἴργειν Τεῦκρος ἐξεφίεται   795

786. ξυρεῖ ἐν χρῷ, literally, "shaves in the skin." "This so cuts to the quick that a certain person will not rejoice."—τινὰ means Tecmessa.

792. οὐκ οἶδα τὴν σὴν πρᾶξιν, Αἴαντος δ᾽ ὅτι . . . . πέρι. Here οἶδα governs both parts of the sentence: "I know nothing about your condition, but about Ajax I know (sc. οἶδα) that I have no hope of him, if he is gone out." The two emphatic words, as opposed to each other, are σὴν and Αἴαντος.

794. Tecmessa replies, καὶ μὴν, "and indeed he is gone out, so that I am distressed beyond measure at what you say." μὴν is used to strengthen the affirmation.—τί φῄς depends on ὠδίνειν.

795. ἐξεφίεται is a stronger

70 ΣΟΦΟΚΛΕΟΥΣ

σκηνῆς ὕπαυλον μηδ᾽ ἀφιέναι μόνον.

ΤΕΚΜΗΣΣΑ.
ποῦ δ᾽ ἐστὶ Τεῦκρος, κἀπὶ τῷ λέγει τάδε;

ΑΓΓΕΛΟΣ.
πάρεστ᾽ ἐκεῖνος ἄρτι· τήνδε δ᾽ ἔξοδον
ὀλεθρίαν Αἴαντος ἐλπίζει φέρειν—

ΤΕΚΜΗΣΣΑ.
οἴμοι τάλαινα, τοῦ ποτ᾽ ἀνθρώπων μαθών;   800

ΑΓΓΕΛΟΣ.
τοῦ Θεστορείου μάντεως, καθ᾽ ἡμέραν
τὴν νῦν, ὅτ᾽ αὐτῷ θάνατον ἢ βίον φέρει.

ΤΕΚΜΗΣΣΑ.
οἲ 'γὼ, φίλοι, πρόστητ᾽ ἀναγκαίας τύχης,
καὶ σπεύσαθ᾽, οἱ μὲν Τεῦκρον ἐν τάχει μολεῖν,

expression than ἐφίεται—" he strictly charges you to keep him within the tent, and not to leave him to himself."

798—802.
πάρεστ᾽ ἐκεῖνος ἄρτι· τήνδε δ᾽ ἔξοδον
ὀλεθρίαν Αἴαντος ἐλπίζει φέρειν—
. . . . φέρει.

The manner in which ὀλεθρίαν is usually taken to be a predicate of ἔξοδον is unsatisfactory, for the order of the words seems to show that it is only a descriptive epithet of that noun. What appears to be the most obvious method of construing the passage, τήνδε δ᾽ ἔξοδον ὀλεθρίαν Αἴαντος ἐλπίζει φέρειν—, is to take it as an unfinished sentence thus: "he is just arrived, and he fears that this destructive going out of Ajax brings—." Tecmessa, greatly alarmed at the grave emphasis which the messenger lays on the death-boding expression, τήνδε δ᾽ ἐξ. ὀλεθρίαν, and at once anticipating the worst consequences of his going out of his tent, even death itself, interrupts him with the question, "From whom having heard it?" Then follows a sentence which is so difficult to be construed, that the reading is rightly considered to be corrupt. ὅτ᾽ for ὅτε is inexplicable. Yet I think that there cannot be a doubt that what was meant to be said was—

"that this day
Would bring or certain death or life secure."—Dale.

As if it had been written, τήνδ᾽ ἡμέραν τὴν νῦν ἐκείνῳ θάνατον ἢ βίον φέρειν. Cf. Il. 13. 828, ὡς νῦν ἡμέρη ἥδε κακὸν φέρει Ἀργείοισι.

ΑΙΑΣ.

οἱ δ᾽ ἑσπέρους ἀγκῶνας, οἱ δ᾽ ἀντηλίους 805
ζητεῖτ᾽ ἰόντες τἀνδρὸς ἔξοδον κακήν.
ἔγνωκα γὰρ δὴ φωτὸς ἠπατημένη
καὶ τῆς παλαιᾶς χάριτος ἐκβεβλημένη.
οἴμοι, τί δράσω, τέκνον; οὐχ ἱδρυτέον.
ἀλλ᾽ εἶμι κἀγὼ κεῖσ᾽ ὅποιπερ ἂν σθένω. 810
χωρῶμεν, ἐγκονῶμεν, οὐχ ἕδρας ἀκμή.
σώζειν θέλοντες ἄνδρα γ᾽ ὃς σπεύδει θανεῖν.

ΧΟΡΟΣ.

χωρεῖν ἕτοιμος, κοὐ λόγῳ δείξω μόνον.
τάχος γὰρ ἔργου καὶ ποδῶν ἅμ᾽ ἕψεται.

ΑΙΑΣ.

ὁ μὲν σφαγεὺς ἕστηκεν ᾗ τομώτατος 815
γένοιτ᾽ ἄν, εἴ τῳ καὶ λογίζεσθαι σχολὴ,
δῶρον μὲν ἀνδρὸς Ἕκτορος ξένων ἐμοὶ
μάλιστα μισηθέντος, ἐχθίστου θ᾽ ὁρᾶν.
πέπηγε δ᾽ ἐν γῇ πολεμίᾳ τῇ Τρῳάδι,
σιδηροβρῶτι θηγάνη νεακονής· 820
ἔπηξα δ᾽ αὐτὸν εὖ περιστείλας ἐγώ,
εὐνούστατον τῷδ᾽ ἀνδρὶ διὰ τάχους θανεῖν.
οὕτω μὲν εὐσκευοῦμεν· ἐκ δὲ τῶνδέ μοι
σὺ πρῶτος, ὦ Ζεῦ, καὶ γὰρ εἰκὸς, ἄρκεσον.
αἰτήσομαι δέ σ᾽ οὐ μακρὸν γέρας λαχεῖν. 825
πέμψον τιν᾽ ἡμῖν ἄγγελον, κακὴν φάτιν
Τεύκρῳ φέροντα, πρῶτος ὥς με βαστάσῃ

811, 812. χωρῶμεν... θανεῖν. Tecmessa having expressed the greatest fear of the fatal consequences of the going out of Ajax, concludes with these words:

"Away, away,
Now is the time to act, who fain would snatch From death the man, who only hastes to die."—*Dale*.

θέλοντες depends on χωρῶμεν.—ἄνδρα γ᾽. The particle γε points to a peculiarity in the man. "He is a man who is actually hastening to death. If then you would save him, there is not a moment to be lost."

72   ΣΟΦΟΚΛΕΟΥΣ

πεπτῶτα τῷδε περὶ νεορράντῳ ξίφει,
καὶ μὴ πρὸς ἐχθρῶν του κατοπτευθεὶς πάρος
ῥιφθῶ κυσὶν πρόβλητος οἰωνοῖς θ' ἕλωρ.   830
τοσαῦτά σ', ὦ Ζεῦ, προστρέπω, καλῶ θ' ἅμα
πομπαῖον Ἑρμῆν χθόνιον εὖ με κοιμίσαι,
ξὺν ἀσφαδάστῳ καὶ ταχεῖ πηδήματι
πλευρὰν διαρρήξαντα τῷδε φασγάνῳ.
καλῶ δ' ἀρωγοὺς τὰς ἀεί τε παρθένους   835
ἀεί θ' ὁρώσας πάντα τὰν βροτοῖς πάθη,
σεμνὰς Ἐρινῦς τανύποδας, μαθεῖν ἐμὲ
πρὸς τῶν Ἀτρειδῶν ὡς διόλλυμαι τάλας.
καί σφας κακοὺς κάκιστα καὶ πανωλέθρους
ξυναρπάσειαν, ὥσπερ εἰσορῶσ' ἐμὲ   840
[αὐτοσφαγῆ πίπτοντα, τὼς αὐτοσφαγεῖς
πρὸς τῶν φιλίστων ἐκγόνων ὀλοίατο.]

837. μαθεῖν ἐμέ. The infin. depends on καλῶ. "I call on the venerable Erinyes *to consider me,* how" &c. The comp. καταμανθάνειν is sometimes used in this sense, as in Xen. Cyr. 7. 5. 2, Xen. An. 3. 1. 4, and N. T. Matth. 6. 28.

839, 840. καί σφας . . . ὥσπερ εἰσορῶσ' ἐμέ. "And *them,* as being most base, may they seize and make them to be as utterly destroyed as they see *me* to be." —πανωλέθρους must, I think, be taken as proleptic, in the same manner as ὀλέθριον must be taken in v. 403—" the warlike goddess afflicts me, a miserably ruined man," that is, she makes me such by her affliction. So here Ajax prays that the Erinyes may bring the Atridae to as extreme a misery and ruin as Athene had brought himself.— σφας and ἐμέ stand in opposition to each other.

841, 842. αὐτοσφαγῆ . . . The arguments which are usually brought forward to prove the spuriousness of these two lines are abundantly sufficient for the purpose. It is noticeable, however, that those arguments do not affect in the slightest degree the genuineness of the two preceding ones, which are nevertheless rejected by some eminent critics as spurious, without any cause whatever being assigned by them for their rejection. The two preceding verses not only form a complete sentence in themselves, for ὥσπερ εἰσ. ἐμὲ is equivalent to ὥσπερ εἰσ. ἐμὲ πανώλεθρον, but if anything further be added, a copula is required before ὥσπερ. Moreover a severe imprecation seems in this place specially required against the Atridae before proceeding to any general mention of the whole army.

ΑΙΑΣ.

ἴτ', ὦ ταχεῖαι ποίνιμοί τ' Ἐρινύες,
γεύεσθε, μὴ φείδεσθε πανδήμου στρατοῦ.
σὺ δ', ὦ τὸν αἰπὺν οὐρανὸν διφρηλατῶν   845
Ἥλιε, πατρῴαν τὴν ἐμὴν ὅταν χθόνα
ἴδῃς, ἐπισχὼν χρυσόνωτον ἡνίαν
ἄγγειλον ἄτας τὰς ἐμὰς μόρον τ' ἐμὸν
γέροντι πατρὶ τῇ τε δυστήνῳ τροφῷ.
ἦ που τάλαινα, τήνδ' ὅταν κλύῃ φάτιν,   850
ἥσει μέγαν κωκυτὸν ἐν πάσῃ πόλει.
ἀλλ' οὐδὲν ἔργον ταῦτα θρηνεῖσθαι μάτην,
ἀλλ' ἀρκτέον τὸ πρᾶγμα σὺν τάχει τινί.
ὦ Θάνατε Θάνατε, νῦν μ' ἐπίσκεψαι μολών·
καίτοι σὲ μὲν κἀκεῖ προσαυδήσω ξυνών.   855
σὲ δ', ὦ φαεννῆς ἡμέρας τὸ νῦν σέλας,
καὶ τὸν διφρευτὴν Ἥλιον προσεννέπω,
πανύστατον δὴ κοὔποτ' αὖθις ὕστερον.
ὦ φέγγος, ὦ γῆς ἱρὸν οἰκείας πέδον
Σαλαμῖνος, ὦ πατρῷον ἑστίας βάθρον,   860
κλειναί τ' Ἀθῆναι, καὶ τὸ σύντροφον γένος,
κρῆναί τε ποταμοί θ' οἵδε, καὶ τὰ Τρωϊκὰ
πεδία προσαυδῶ, χαίρετ', ὦ τροφῆς ἐμοί·
τοῦθ' ὑμῖν Αἴας τοὔπος ὕστατον θροεῖ·

853. σὺν τάχει τινί, "with a certain degree of quickness," or "with a little expedition." Ajax says this, because he had taken a good deal of time in fixing his sword, looking at it afterwards, and seeing that all was well arranged. He then stops to make certain reflections on its being the gift of an enemy; then invokes Jove and Hermes, then the dread Furies to avenge his death on the Atridae, and lastly the Sun to reveal the manner of his death to his aged parents; and while reflecting on the bitter grief it would occasion to them, he breaks off with saying, "But it is no use to dwell any longer on this painful subject; I must begin the work with a little haste." Even after this he waits to cast one longing lingering look on the scenes around him, and bids them a long and last adieu. There was no excessive or vehement haste in the matter, for nothing could be more deliberate and reflective than the death of Ajax.

74 ΣΟΦΟΚΛΕΟΥΣ

τὰ δ' ἄλλ' ἐν "Αιδου τοῖς κάτω μυθήσομαι. 865
ΗΜΙΧΟΡΙΟΝ.
πόνος πόνῳ πόνον φέρει.
πᾶ πᾶ
πᾶ γὰρ οὐκ ἔβαν ἐγώ;
κοὐδεὶς ἐπίσταταί με συμμαθεῖν τόπος.
ἰδού, 870
δοῦπον αὖ κλύω τινά.
ΗΜΙΧΟΡΙΟΝ.
ἡμῶν γε ναὸς κοινόπλουν ὁμιλίαν.
ΗΜΙΧΟΡΙΟΝ.
τί οὖν δή;
ΗΜΙΧΟΡΙΟΝ.
πᾶν ἐστίβηται πλευρὸν ἕσπερον νεῶν.
ΗΜΙΧΟΡΙΟΝ.
ἔχεις οὖν; 875
ΗΜΙΧΟΡΙΟΝ.
πόνου γε πλῆθος, κοὐδὲν εἰς ὄψιν πλέον.
ΗΜΙΧΟΡΙΟΝ.
ἀλλ' οὐδὲ μὲν δὴ τὴν ἀφ' ἡλίου βολῶν
κέλευθον ἀνὴρ οὐδαμοῦ δηλοῖ φανείς.
ΧΟΡΟΣ.
τίς ἂν δῆτά μοι, τίς ἂν φιλοπόνων στρ. 879
ἁλιαδᾶν ἔχων ἀμφ' ἀύπνους ἄγρας,
ἢ τίς Ὀλυμπιάδων θεᾶν, ἢ ῥυτῶν

869. κοὐδεὶς ἐπίσταταί με συμμαθεῖν τόπος. This may be construed, "and yet no place knows him, so that I may share with it in learning where he is." A place in poetic language may be said to know something about a man if it retains any traces of him or of his footsteps. In the poetic imagery of Ps. 103 man in his most flourishing state is likened to the flower of the field —" for the wind passeth over it and it is gone, and *the place thereof shall know it* no more."

ΑΙΑΣ.

Βοσπορίων ποταμῶν, τὸν ὠμόθυμον 885
εἴ ποθι πλαζόμενον λεύσσων
ἀπύοι; σχέτλια γὰρ
ἐμέ γε τὸν μακρῶν ἀλάταν πόνων
οὐρίῳ μὴ πελάσαι δρόμῳ,
ἀλλ' ἀμενηνὸν ἄνδρα μὴ λεύσσειν ὅπου. 890

ΤΕΚΜΗΣΣΑ.
ἰώ μοί μοι.

ΧΟΡΟΣ.
τίνος βοὴ πάραυλος ἐξέβη νάπους;

ΤΕΚΜΗΣΣΑ.
ἰὼ τλάμων.

ΧΟΡΟΣ.
τὴν δουρίληπτον δύσμορον νύμφην ὁρῶ
Τέκμησσαν, οἴκτῳ τῷδε συγκεκραμένην. 895

ΤΕΚΜΗΣΣΑ.
ᾤχωκ', ὄλωλα, διαπεπόρθημαι, φίλοι.

ΧΟΡΟΣ.
τί δ' ἔστιν;

ΤΕΚΜΗΣΣΑ.
Αἴας ὅδ' ἡμῖν ἀρτίως νεοσφαγὴς
κεῖται, κρυφαίῳ φασγάνῳ περιπτυχής.

890. ἀλλ' ἀμενηνὸν ἄνδρα μὴ λεύσσειν ὅπου. The speaker is so dispirited on account of the ill success of his search after Ajax, and is become so unhopeful of meeting with him alive, after having heard of his predicted doom on that present day, that he anticipates the fulfilment of it, and speaks of him as one who was already dead. "It is a wretched thing for me, after so much toilsome wandering, that I should not be successful in approaching him, and can nowhere find the lifeless man." He was thrown into such despair that he rather expected to meet with him dead than alive.

899. κρυφαίῳ φασγάνῳ περιπτυχής. "Enfolding the hidden sword," making, so to speak, his body a shroud to the sword. Cf. 915, περιπτυχεῖ φάρει, "with a winding-sheet."

76   ΣΟΦΟΚΛΕΟΤΣ

ΧΟΡΟΣ.
ὤμοι ἐμῶν νόστων·   900
ὤμοι, κατέπεφνες, ἄναξ, *
τόνδε συνναύταν, ὦ τάλας·
ὦ ταλαίφρον γύναι.

ΤΕΚΜΗΣΣΑ.
ὡς ὧδε τοῦδ᾽ ἔχοντος αἰάζειν πάρα.

ΧΟΡΟΣ.
τίνος ποτ᾽ ἄρ᾽ ἔρξε χειρὶ δύσμορος;   905

ΤΕΚΜΗΣΣΑ.
αὐτὸς πρὸς αὑτοῦ· δῆλον. ἐν γάρ οἱ χθονὶ
πηκτὸν τόδ᾽ ἔγχος περιπετὲς κατηγορεῖ.

905. ἔπραξε has been changed into ἔρξε for the sake of metre. That question of metre is relegated to the Appendix.

906, 907. I construe this, "for this sword fixed in the ground, *which has run into him*, convicts him." The word περιπετὲς is generally believed to be used here in a passive sense, "the sword on which he fell," which is the same as saying "the sword which was fallen upon." It is to be observed that Eustathius speaks of it thus: Σοφοκλῆς ἔγχος περιπετὲς εἰπεῖν ἐτόλμησεν, ᾧ περιέπεσεν Αἴας. These words, ἐτόλμησεν εἰπεῖν, plainly show that he considered it to be a most extraordinary circumstance that Sophocles should have used it in a passive sense; and if he really did, it is certainly an extraordinary use of this word, for none of the other compounds of a similar kind are ever used passively, as προπετὴς, ὑψιπετὴς, χαμαιπετὴς, εὐπετὴς, δυσπετὴς, and many others. I believe that it was intended by the poet to convey the idea of a sword which had fallen *into* him, or as we should rather express it in English, a sword which had run into him. Dindorf quotes Joann. Chrysost. vol. iii. p. 85 A, ἑαυτῷ τὸ ξίφος περιέπειρε, "he pierced the sword *into* his own body." Lobeck quotes Aelian, Hist. Anim. 15, c. 10, ἄγκιστρα περιπαγέντα τοῖσιν ἰχθύσι, "hooks pierced *into* the fishes." Why then may not οἱ ἔγχος περιπετὲς be "a sword which has run *into* him"? In Eur. An. 982, ἐπειδὴ περιπετεῖς ἔχεις τύχας, it seems much more probable that the word was used actively, "since you are suffering calamities that *have fallen* upon you," than passively, "calamities which *have been fallen upon* by you." Paley in his note on the passage quotes Photius: περιπετῆ γενέσθαι, περιπεπτωκέναι, an explanation which evidently gives it an active sense—to become one that *has fallen*, not one that *has been fallen upon*.

ΑΙΑΣ. 77

ΧΟΡΟΣ.

ὤμοι ἐμᾶς ἄτας, οἷος ἄρ' αἱμάχθης, ἄφαρκτος φίλων·
ἐγὼ δ' ὁ πάντα κωφὸς, ὁ πάντ' ἄϊδρις, κατημέλησα.
πᾶ πᾶ 911
κεῖται ὁ δυστράπελος, δυσώνυμος Αἴας;

ΤΕΚΜΗΣΣΑ.

οὔτοι θεατός· ἀλλά νιν περιπτυχεῖ 915
φάρει καλύψω τῷδε παμπήδην, ἐπεὶ
οὐδεὶς ἂν, ὅστις καὶ φίλος, τλαίη βλέπειν

910. οἷος ἄρ' αἱμάχθης. "Alas for my ill fate! alone then, unguarded by thy friends, thou didst fall into this bloody death, whilst I (who should have kept you from it), all unconscious and ignorant of your state, disregarded you."—οἷος is the right reading, not οἶος. If the whole tenor of the sentence did not show it, that one little word ἄρ' is sufficient to decide the matter. Teucer having heard how it was that Ajax had contrived his death, reflects on the manner of it, and says, "I see *then* (ἄρ') how it was: you were left to go out alone; you had no friends to watch and guard you; and I who should have taken care of you, alas for my ill fortune! knew nothing at all about your sad and miserable condition. See note on v. 925.

917. οὐδεὶς ἂν, ὅστις καὶ φίλος, τλαίη βλέπειν. The usual and right way of construing this is, "No one who is also a friend could bear to look on the mangled corpse." This is in accordance with the common feelings of mankind. A ferocious enemy might gaze on it with delight, and cast it out uncovered; but no one who had a tender regard for the deceased would not rather veil it even from his own sight with a decent robe. There is, however, a way of construing it, which has the authority of Lobeck, Dindorf, and others, and is as follows: "No one, *even though* he should be a friend, could bear to look on it." This way implies that a friend could bear to look on it better than any other person. If those who take this view of it could only adduce one instance where ὅστις καὶ, being put together, the καὶ does not belong to ὅστις, but is used simply to emphasize the word which follows it, such one instance would have more weight in determining the question than any mere expression of their opinion; but no such instance has been met with. On the other hand, instances of ὅστις καὶ being taken together appear to be as frequently met with as we find them put together. Cf. Eur. Ion 232, πάντα θεᾶσθ', ὅ τι καὶ θέμις, ὄμμασι. Eur. Hel. 1200, ἥκει γὰρ ὅστις καὶ τάδ' ἀγγέλλει σαφῆ; O. C. 183, ὅ τι καὶ πόλις τέτροφεν ἄφιλον. Trach. 726, οὐδ' ἐλπὶς, ἥτις καὶ θράσος τι προξενεῖ.

78 ΣΟΦΟΚΛΕΟΤΣ

φυσῶντ' ἄνω πρὸς ῥῖνας, ἔκ τε φοινίας
πληγῆς μελανθὲν αἷμ' ἀπ' οἰκείας σφαγῆς.
οἴμοι, τί δράσω; τίς σε βαστάσει φίλων;   920
ποῦ Τεῦκρος; ὡς ἀκμαῖος, εἰ βαίη, μόλοι,
πεπτῶτ' ἀδελφὸν τόνδε συγκαθαρμόσαι.
ὦ δύσμορ' Αἶας, οἶος ὢν οἴως ἔχεις,
ὡς καὶ παρ' ἐχθροῖς ἄξιος θρήνων τυχεῖν.

ΧΟΡΟΣ.
ἔμελλες, τάλας, ἔμελλες χρόνῳ   ἀντ. 925
στερεόφρων ἄρ' ὧδ' ἐξανύσειν κακὰν
μοῖραν ἀπειρεσίων πόνων. τοῖά μοι
πάννυχα καὶ φαέθοντ' ἀνεστέναζες   930
ὠμόφρων ἐχθοδόπ' Ἀτρείδαις
οὐλίῳ σὺν πάθει.
μέγας ἄρ' ἦν ἐκεῖνος ἄρχων χρόνος
πημάτων, ἦμος ἀριστόχειρ   935
* * * * ὅπλων ἔκειτ' ἀγὼν πέρι.

ΤΕΚΜΗΣΣΑ.
ἰώ μοί μοι.

921. ὡς ἀκμαῖος, εἰ βαίη, μόλοι. This has been construed in various ways. Elmsley's is, "Oh! that he might come, if he comes at all, in good time." This undoubtedly is the required sense. There could be no reasonable doubt that Teucer would come, but the anxious fear of the friends of the deceased was, that he might not come in good time to prevent the ignominious treatment of the dead body by his enemies.—ὡς, with a verb in the optative, is sometimes used to express a fervent wish. El. 1226, ὡς τὰ λοίπ' ἔχοις ἀεί.

925—927. "Thou wert resolved, wretched man, thou wert resolved then in course of time to terminate thine evil lot of countless woes." χρόνῳ, "in course of time." From the period of the recovery of his senses, Ajax had been meditating this suicide, v. 326, and from that time forth he gave on frequent occasions intimations of his purpose. The Chorus reflecting on all this says, "I see then (ἄρ') it was no sudden impulse of the mind. However circumstances might stand in the way of this self-murder, yet you were determined to accomplish it in course of time, whenever you could contrive an opportunity of effecting it, in the absence of your friends."

ΑΙΑΣ.

ΧΟΡΟΣ.
χωρεῖ πρὸς ἧπαρ, οἶδα, γενναία δύη.
ΤΕΚΜΗΣΣΑ.
ἰώ μοί μοι.
ΧΟΡΟΣ.
οὐδέν σ' ἀπιστῶ καὶ δὶς οἰμῶξαι, γύναι, 940
τοιοῦδ' ἀποβλαφθεῖσαν ἀρτίως φίλου.
ΤΕΚΜΗΣΣΑ.
σοὶ μὲν δοκεῖν ταῦτ' ἔστ', ἐμοὶ δ' ἄγαν φρονεῖν.
ΧΟΡΟΣ.
ξυναυδῶ.
ΤΕΚΜΗΣΣΑ.
οἴμοι, τέκνον, πρὸς οἷα δουλείας ζυγὰ
χωροῦμεν, οἷοι νῷν ἐφεστᾶσι σκοποί. 945
ΧΟΡΟΣ.
ὤμοι, ἀναλγήτων
δισσῶν ἐθρόησας ἄναυδον
ἔργον Ἀτρειδᾶν τῷδ' ἄχει.
ἀλλ' ἀπείργοι θεός.
ΤΕΚΜΗΣΣΑ.
οὐκ ἂν τάδ' ἔστη τῇδε, μὴ θεῶν μέτα. 950
ΧΟΡΟΣ.
ἄγαν ὑπερβριθὲς ἄχθος ἤνυσαν.
ΤΕΚΜΗΣΣΑ.
τοιόνδε μέντοι Ζηνὸς ἡ δεινὴ θεὸς
Παλλὰς φυτεύει πῆμ' Ὀδυσσέως χάριν.
ΧΟΡΟΣ.
ἦ ῥα κελαινώπαν θυμὸν ἐφυβρίζει πολύτλας ἀνὴρ,

954—960.
ἦ ῥα κελαινώπαν .... Ἀτρεῖδαι.

"The chief of many toils
In his dark soul will doubtless mock
Our tears with bitterest scorn,
And laugh insulting at the woes we bear
For deeds in frenzy wrought!
So too the brother-kings
Hearing the welcome tale." *Dale.*

ΣΟΦΟΚΛΕΟΥΣ

γελᾷ δὲ τοῖσδε μαινομένοις ἄχεσιν πολὺν γέλωτα,
 φεῦ φεῦ,
ξύν τε διπλοῖ βασιλῆς κλύοντες Ἀτρεῖδαι.   960

ΤΕΚΜΗΣΣΑ.

οἱ δ᾽ οὖν γελώντων κἀπιχαιρόντων κακοῖς
τοῖς τοῦδ᾽. ἴσως τοι, κεἰ βλέποντα μὴ 'πόθουν,
θανόντ᾽ ἂν οἰμώξειαν ἐν χρείᾳ δορός.

κελαινώπαν θυμὸν seems to be very properly translated "in his dark soul," and to mean that Odysseus was a great dissembler, and that he was secretly delighted at hearing the fatal result of Ajax's madness; for the Chorus is unsparing in his abuse of Odysseus as well as of the two Atridae. We must be careful, however, to distinguish his character as given by the poet himself from that which a partisan of Ajax ascribes to him. According to the description given by the poet himself of the part which Odysseus takes in this drama, there is not a word which he says, or a thing which he does, which is other than that which a wise, just, and honourable man would say or do on a like occasion. In the opening of the play he is seen tracking the foot-prints of Ajax, and sometimes looking into the tent to see if he is within; but it is simply with the view of finding out the real facts of the case as regards the slaughter of the public cattle; and when he is informed of them, instead of exhibiting the slightest feeling of malevolence against the man who had been his personal foe, he says, v. 121, "Alas! I pity him. E'en in a foe I pity such distress." Francklin. After this he appears no more till the last scene. Then it was that having heard from afar the clamorous strife that had arisen between the Atridae and Teucer, he comes among them, and in a most forcible speech he sets before Agamemnon the impiety and injustice he would be guilty of, if he forbade the burial of so brave a warrior; and in a further talk with him, having at length overcome his reluctance to the burial of Ajax, he offers his own most hearty services to Teucer in taking part with him in the burial, and declares that he is now become as much the friend of Ajax as before he was his enemy. All this shows that the Chorus had taken a wrong view of Odysseus. Be it observed, however, that in the epithet πολύτλας as applied to him, nothing reproachful could have been intended. It was simply a designation of the person, his name having not been mentioned. In the Il. and Od. of Homer, the three words, πολύτλας δῖος Ὀδυσσεὺς, occur more than thirty times, and never once is the epithet πολύτλας applied to any other than Odysseus, and then always in combination with that honourable one δῖος. It is therefore always used in a good sense.

ΑΙΑΣ. 81

οἱ γὰρ κακοὶ γνώμαισι τἀγαθὸν χεροῖν
ἔχοντες οὐκ ἴσασι, πρίν τις ἐκβάλῃ. 965
ἐμοὶ πικρὸς τέθνηκεν ἢ κείνοις γλυκύς,
αὑτῷ δὲ τερπνός. ὧν γὰρ ἠράσθη τυχεῖν
ἐκτήσαθ᾽ αὑτῷ, θάνατον, ὅνπερ ἤθελεν.
τί δῆτα τοῦδ᾽ ἐπεγγελῷεν ἂν κάτα;
θεοῖς τέθνηκεν οὗτος, οὐ κείνοισιν, οὔ. 970
πρὸς ταῦτ᾽ Ὀδυσσεὺς ἐν κενοῖς ὑβριζέτω.
Αἴας γὰρ αὐτοῖς οὐκέτ᾽ ἐστὶν, ἀλλ᾽ ἐμοὶ
λιπὼν ἀνίας καὶ γόους διοίχεται.

ΤΕΥΚΡΟΣ.

ἰώ μοί μοι.

966. ἐμοὶ πικρὸς τέθνηκεν ἤ. This is an elliptical expression for μᾶλλον ἤ. See Matth. 457, obs. 1, where he quotes Hdt. 9. 26, ἡμέας δίκαιον ἔχειν τὸ ἕτερον κέρας, ἤπερ 'Αθηναίους. Thuc. 6. 21, αἰσχρὸν δὲ βιασθέντας ἀπελθεῖν, ἢ ὕστερον ἐπιμεταπέμπεσθαι, τὸ πρῶτον ἀσκέπτως βουλευσαμένους. Bos adduces other examples, as the following: Il. 11. 117, βούλομ᾽ ἐγὼ λαὸν σόον ἔμμεναι, ἢ ἀπολέσθαι. Theognis: βούλεο δ᾽ εὐσεβέως ὀλίγοις σὺν χρήμασιν οἰκεῖν, | ἢ πλουτεῖν ἀδίκως χρήματα πασάμενος. Longinus, Sec. 35, τοῖς ἁμαρτήμασι περιττεύει, ἢ ταῖς ἀρεταῖς λείπεται. Il. 17. 331. N. T. Luc. 15. 7; 17. 2; 18. 14; 1 Cor. 14. 19.

970. θεοῖς τέθνηκεν. "The death of this man has been occasioned by the gods, not by them." Not only was the madness of Ajax, which issued in his death, inflicted on him by the goddess Athene, but his very death was the direct effect of her continued persecution: v. 756.—θεοῖς is the dative of the instrument.

971, 972. Αἴας γὰρ αὐτοῖς οὐκέτ᾽ ἐστὶν, ἀλλ᾽ ἐμοί. The very position of the pers. pronouns, αὐτοῖς and ἐμοί, shows that they are put antithetically to each other. The fact is, the sentence refers back to the preceding one, which is only a continuation of what Tecmessa had said at the beginning of her speech. We may therefore explain the antithesis thus: "for Ajax is *to them* no more, however much they may laugh and rejoice over his misfortunes (v. 961); *but to me* it is altogether a different thing: he has left to me nothing but miseries and lamentations." This is an instance where the participle with its adjuncts conveys the principal idea, and where the verb διοίχεται might have been omitted altogether, if the participle λιπὼν had been made a verb. Cf. vv. 106—110, θανεῖν οὔ τί πω θέλω, πρὶν ἂν . . . . μάστιγι πρῶτον νῶτα φοινιχθεὶς θάνῃ, where θάνῃ ought to be utterly ignored, except as introducing the participle with its adjuncts.

AJ. S. G

82   ΣΟΦΟΚΛΕΟΥΣ

                        ΧΟΡΟΣ.
σίγησον.   αὐδὴν γὰρ δοκῶ Τεύκρου κλύειν   975
βοῶντος ἄτης τῆσδ᾽ ἐπίσκοπον μέλος.
                        ΤΕΥΚΡΟΣ.
ὦ φίλτατ᾽ Αἴας, ὦ ξύναιμον ὄμμ᾽ ἐμοὶ,
ἆρ᾽ ἠμπόληκας, ὥσπερ ἡ φάτις κρατεῖ;
                        ΧΟΡΟΣ.
ὄλωλεν ἀνὴρ, Τεῦκρε, τοῦτ᾽ ἐπίστασο.
                        ΤΕΥΚΡΟΣ.
ὤμοι βαρείας ἆρα τῆς ἐμῆς τύχης.   980
                        ΧΟΡΟΣ.
ὡς ὧδ᾽ ἐχόντων
                        ΤΕΥΚΡΟΣ.
                 ὦ τάλας ἐγὼ, τάλας.
                        ΧΟΡΟΣ.
πάρα στενάζειν,
                        ΤΕΥΚΡΟΣ.
                 ὦ περισφερχὲς πάθος.
                        ΧΟΡΟΣ.
ἄγαν γε, Τεῦκρε.
                        ΤΕΥΚΡΟΣ.
                 φεῦ τάλας. τί γὰρ τέκνον

976. ἐπίσκοπον. "A strain that has regard (or respect) to this disaster." "Interpreteris non absurde: quale debet ejus esse, qui talem caedem conspicit. Aesch. Eum. 862, ὁποῖα νίκης μὴ κακῆς ἐπίσκοπα." Musgrave. It was a mournful strain of one who was contemplating the self-inflicted death of his dearest friend.

978. ἆρ᾽ ἠμπόληκας. "Hast thou made such a bargain as men say thou hast?" Cf. Trach. 537, παρεισδέδεγμαι ... λωβητὸν ἐμπόλημα, where the noun is used in a bad sense, as the verb is here. With respect to the intransitive use of the verb, Lobeck compares Hipp. de Morb. 4. 12, p. 608, ἢν τοῦ ἀποπάτου μὴ διαχωρέοντος κρατέῃ μία τῶν ἄλλων ἰκμὰς, κάλλιον ἐμπολήσει—melius sese habebit. Strange as this expression may seem to be, perhaps it is not a whit more so than the idiomatic phrase into which it may be translated: "the man will *get* better."

ΑΙΑΣ.

τὸ τοῦδε ποῦ μοι γῆς κυρεῖ τῆς Τρῳάδος;
ΧΟΡΟΣ.
μόνος παρὰ σκηναῖσιν. 985
ΤΕΥΚΡΟΣ.
οὐχ ὅσον τάχος
δῆτ᾽ αὐτὸν ἄξεις δεῦρο, μή τις ὡς κενῆς
σκύμνον λεαίνης δυσμενῶν ἀναρπάσῃ;
ἴθ᾽, ἐγκόνει, σύγκαμνε. τοῖς θανοῦσί τοι
φιλοῦσι πάντες κειμένοις ἐπεγγελᾶν.
ΧΟΡΟΣ.
καὶ μὴν ἔτι ζῶν, Τεῦκρε, τοῦδέ σοι μέλειν 990
ἐφίεθ᾽ ἁνὴρ κεῖνος, ὥσπερ οὖν μέλει.
ΤΕΥΚΡΟΣ.
ὦ τῶν ἁπάντων δὴ θεαμάτων ἐμοὶ
ἄλγιστον ὧν προσεῖδον ὀφθαλμοῖς ἐγώ,
ὁδός θ᾽ ὁδῶν πασῶν ἀνιάσασα δὴ
μάλιστα τοὐμὸν σπλάγχνον, ἣν δὴ νῦν ἔβην, 995
ὦ φίλτατ᾽ Αἴας, τὸν σὸν ὡς ἐπῃσθόμην
μόρον διώκων κἀξιχνοσκοπούμενος.
ὀξεῖα γάρ σου βάξις ὡς θεοῦ τινὸς

986. ὡς κενῆς σ. λεαίνης. Tecmessa is here represented by this simile as *desolate*, with reference to her husband rather than her son; and κενῆς λεαίνης does not mean "a lioness robbed of her young," but "a deserted lioness, whose mate has been destroyed." Admitting it to be true that such a deserted lioness would still be powerful enough to protect her young, and the simile in this respect would have no similitude to the case of Tecmessa, yet most persons, I think, will agree with Wunder in what he says on this point:

"Tamen haec dissimilitudo audientium animos ante praeterlabitur quam percepta est, quippe quibus verba ipsa nihil praeter viduitatis et orbitatis notionem subjiciant, sic ut hoc solum in cogitatione haereat et obversetur,—MATER A MARITO DESTITUTA, FILIUS FORTISSIMO PATRE ORBATUS."

998. ὡς θεοῦ τινός.

"A sad report of thee as by some god
Was quickly blazoned through the Argive host."—*Dale.*

Soph. introduces Teucer as at-

84 ΣΟΦΟΚΛΕΟΥΣ

διῆλθ' Ἀχαιοὺς πάντας ὡς οἴχει θανών.
ἀγὼ κλύων δείλαιος ἐκποδὼν μὲν ὢν   1000
ὑπεστέναζον, νῦν δ' ὁρῶν ἀπόλλυμαι.
οἴμοι.
ἴθ' ἐκκάλυψον, ὡς ἴδω τὸ πᾶν κακόν.
ὦ δυσθέατον ὄμμα καὶ τόλμης πικρᾶς,
ὅσας ἀνίας μοι κατασπείρας φθίνεις.   1005
ποῖ γὰρ μολεῖν μοι δυνατόν, ἐς ποίους βροτοὺς,
τοῖς σοῖς ἀρήξαντ' ἐν πόνοισι μηδαμοῦ;
ἦ πού με Τελαμών, σὸς πατὴρ ἐμός θ' ἅμα,
δέξαιτ' ἂν εὐπρόσωπος ἵλεώς τ' ἴσως
χωροῦντ' ἄνευ σοῦ. πῶς γὰρ οὔχ; ὅτῳ πάρα   1010

tributing the sudden and rapid rumour of Ajax's death to the influence of some god, in order to show that the prayer uttered by him in v. 846 was fulfilled.

1004. ὦ δυσθέατον ὄμμα. "O sight most grievous to behold, and one of bitter rashness." The word ὄμμα can hardly mean the form of Ajax, but rather the ghastly sight or appearance of his form. Cf. v. 992, and Aesch. Prom. 69, ὁρᾷς θέαμα δυσθέατον ὄμμασιν.

1005. ὅσας ἀνίας μοι κατασπείρας φθίνεις. "How many woes having sown for me hast thou perished." I construe the passage thus literally, in order to show that φθίνεις is used of one who had died a violent death by his own hand. In like manner in v. 405 it appears to be used of the cattle which Ajax had slain in the field. See note on 405.

1010. πῶς γὰρ οὔχ; i. e. πῶς γὰρ οὔ με δέξαιτ' ἂν εὐπρόσωπος ἵλεώς τ' ἴσως;—πῶς γὰρ οὔκ; always refers to the preceding words, and assents to them. Cf.

O. T. 937, ἥδοιο μὲν, πῶς δ' οὐκ ἄν; El. 865, ἄσκοπος ἁ λώβα. πῶς γὰρ οὔκ; Aesch. Ag. ἔστιν· τί δ' οὐχί; Aesch. Pers. 996, δυσπόλεμον δὴ γένος τὸ Περσᾶν. πῶς δ' οὔ; Accordingly πῶς γὰρ οὔχ; requires to be construed in the same style of derisive irony as the preceding words, "Doubtless Telamon, your father and mine, will receive me with quite as joyous a countenance and as kindly a feeling, when I come to him without you, as if you were with me: *of course he will.* How can it be otherwise with a man whose habitual austerity is such that he does not even smile more pleasantly when all goes well with him?" The very point of the sharp irony is in the words πῶς γ. οὔχ; Wunder however explains them thus: "cur non excipiat me gravi severoque vultu?" Linwood approves of this explanation, and Schneidewin's is to the same effect: στυγνῷ με δέξεται προσώπῳ. The explanation of these eminent critics depends entirely on their own simple assertion,

ΑΙΑΣ.

μηδ' εὐτυχοῦντι μηδὲν ἥδιον γελᾶν.
οὗτος τί κρύψει; ποῖον οὐκ ἐρεῖ κακὸν,
τὸν ἐκ δορὸς γεγῶτα πολεμίου νόθον,
τὸν δειλίᾳ προδόντα καὶ κακανδρίᾳ
σὲ, φίλτατ' Αἴας, ἢ δόλοισιν, ὡς τὰ σὰ   1015
κράτη θανόντος καὶ δόμους νέμοιμι σούς.
τοιαῦτ' ἀνὴρ δύσοργος, ἐν γήρᾳ βαρὺς,
ἐρεῖ, πρὸς οὐδὲν εἰς ἔριν θυμούμενος.
τέλος δ' ἀπωστὸς γῆς ἀπορριφθήσομαι,
δοῦλος λόγοισιν ἀντ' ἐλευθέρου φανείς.   1020
τοιαῦτα μὲν κατ' οἶκον· ἐν Τροίᾳ δέ μοι
πολλοὶ μὲν ἐχθροὶ, παῦρα δ' ὠφελήσιμα.
καὶ ταῦτα πάντα σοῦ θανόντος ηὑρόμην.
οἴμοι, τί δράσω; πῶς σ' ἀποσπάσω πικροῦ
τοῦδ' αἰόλου κνώδοντος, ᾧ τάλας, ὑφ' οὗ   1025
φονέως ἄρ' ἐξέπνευσας; εἶδες ὡς χρόνῳ
ἔμελλέ σ' Ἕκτωρ καὶ θανὼν ἀποφθίσειν;
σκέψασθε, πρὸς θεῶν, τὴν τύχην δυοῖν βροτοῖν.
Ἕκτωρ μὲν, ᾧ δὴ τοῦδ' ἐδωρήθη πάρα,

unsupported by the least shadow of a proof.—ὅτῳ πάρεστι, whose wont it is, μὴ μηδὲν ἥδιον γελᾶν, not at all to smile *more* pleasantly when things go well with him, *than when they go ill with him.*

1022. πολλοὶ μὲν ἐχθροί, παῦρα δ' ὠφελήσιμα. All the MSS. ὠφελήσιμοι, and some παῦροι. ὠφελήσιμα, the conjecture of Johnson, is most probably the original reading, and it, together with παῦρα, was intended perhaps to mean very much the same as παῦροι δ' ὠφελήσιμοι. The description which is given in Il. 8. 266 of the protection which Teucer was wont to receive from him in the field of battle is expressive of much tenderness.

1029—1031. The reason why Sophocles may have deviated from the description in Il. 22. 395, and have followed another tradition, seems to have been, because, according to that other tradition, Hector was tied to the chariot of Achilles with the very girdle which had been given to him by Ajax; whereas in Il. 22. 395 he is said to have been tied with thongs, and there is no mention whatever of the girdle. The poor attempts which Hermann and others have made to correct the passage in Aj. 1029—1031, so as to render it more conformable with Homer's description, do not affect this main point at all.

86 ΣΟΦΟΚΛΕΟΥΣ

ζωστῆρι πρισθεὶς ἱππικῶν ἐξ ἀντύγων   1030
ἐκνάπτετ' αἰὲν, ἔς τ' ἀπέψυξεν βίον·
οὗτος δ' ἐκείνου τήνδε δωρεὰν ἔχων
πρὸς τοῦδ' ὄλωλε θανασίμῳ πεσήματι.
ἆρ' οὐκ Ἐρινὺς τοῦτ' ἐχάλκευσε ξίφος
κἀκεῖνον Ἅιδης, δημιουργὸς ἄγριος;   1035
ἐγὼ μὲν ἂν καὶ ταῦτα καὶ τὰ πάντ' ἀεὶ
φάσκοιμ' ἂν ἀνθρώποισι μηχανᾶν θεούς·
ὅτῳ δὲ μὴ τάδ' ἐστὶν ἐν γνώμῃ φίλα,
κεῖνός τ' ἐκεῖνα στεργέτω, κἀγὼ τάδε.

ΧΟΡΟΣ.

μὴ τεῖνε μακρὰν, ἀλλ' ὅπως κρύψεις τάφῳ   1040
φράζου τὸν ἄνδρα, χὤ τι μυθήσει τάχα.
βλέπω γὰρ ἐχθρὸν φῶτα, καὶ τάχ' ἂν κακοῖς
γελῶν ἃ δὴ κακοῦργος ἐξίκοιτ' ἀνήρ.

ΤΕΥΚΡΟΣ.

τίς δ' ἐστὶν ὅντιν' ἄνδρα προσλεύσσεις στρατοῦ;

ΧΟΡΟΣ.

Μενέλαος, ᾧ δὴ τόνδε πλοῦν ἐστείλαμεν.   1045

ΤΕΥΚΡΟΣ.

ὁρῶ· μαθεῖν γὰρ ἐγγὺς ὢν οὐ δυσπετής.

1030. πρισθείς. It is difficult to see how this word came to mean what it does here, except as explained by L. and S., "to seize with the teeth, to *bind fast*." In the passage quoted by Lobeck and Jebb, Oppian Hal. II. 375, ἔνθα μιν ἀμφιβαλὼν περιηγές ταυτόθεν ὁλκῷ | ἴσχει τ' ἐμπρίει, the word ἐμπρίει can only mean that the net *presses closely* around the fish, without any notion of working into their flesh; and so here πρισθείς seems simply to mean, *bound fast* with the girdle to the circular rim of the chariot.

1043. ἃ δὴ κακ. ἀνήρ, "*as a villain*," or "*like* a villain." See Matth. 486. 4, b, where he refers to Plat. Phaedr. 244 E, ἀλλὰ μὴν νόσων γε καὶ πόνων τῶν μεγίστων, ἃ δὴ παλαιῶν ἐκ μηνιμάτων ποθὲν ἔν τισι τῶν γενῶν . . . ἡ μανία ἀπαλλαγὴν εὕρετο, and Plat. Leg. 6. 778 Α, μή προσπαίζοντας μηδαμῶς οἰκέταις μήτ' οὖν θηλείαις μήτε ἄρρεσιν, ἃ δὴ πρὸς δούλους φιλοῦσι πολλοί.

ΑΙΑΣ.

ΜΕΝΕΛΑΟΣ.
οὗτος, σὲ φωνῶ τόνδε τὸν νεκρὸν χεροῖν
μὴ συγκομίζειν, ἀλλ' ἐᾶν ὅπως ἔχει.

ΤΕΥΚΡΟΣ.
τίνος χάριν τοσόνδ' ἀνήλωσας λόγον;

ΜΕΝΕΛΑΟΣ.
δοκοῦντ' ἐμοὶ, δοκοῦντα δ' ὃς κραίνει στρατοῦ.

ΤΕΥΚΡΟΣ.
οὔκουν ἂν εἴποις ἥντιν' αἰτίαν προθείς; 1051

ΜΕΝΕΛΑΟΣ.
ὁθούνεκ' αὐτὸν ἐλπίσαντες οἴκοθεν
ἄγειν Ἀχαιοῖς ξύμμαχόν τε καὶ φίλον,
ἐξηύρομεν ζητοῦντες ἐχθίω Φρυγῶν·
ὅστις στρατῷ ξύμπαντι βουλεύσας φόνον 1055
νύκτωρ ἐπεστράτευσεν, ὡς ἕλοι δόρει·
κεἰ μὴ θεῶν τις τήνδε πεῖραν ἔσβεσεν,
ἡμεῖς μὲν ἂν τήνδ', ἣν ὅδ' εἴληχεν τύχην,

1049. τίνος χάριν τοσόνδ' ἀνήλωσας λόγον; "For what purpose hast thou wasted on me such an imperious word?" Teucer intimates by this word ἀνήλωσας that he does not mean to pay the slightest heed to his peremptory prohibition of the burial of Ajax. (Dind.)—ἀνάλωσας. "We find ἀνήλωσα in inscriptions which were engraved long before the Attic dialect began to decline from its purity." Elmsley.

1050. δοκοῦντ' ἐμοὶ, δοκοῦντα δ' ὃς κραίνει στρατοῦ. Brief sentences are frequently used in a dialogue. This one, for instance, would seem to be in full, ταῦτ' ἐστὶ δοκοῦντ' ἐμοὶ, δοκοῦντα δ' ἐκείνῳ ὃς κραίνει στρατοῦ. So the following would be, οὔκουν ἂν εἴποις ἥντιν' αἰτίαν προθεὶς (τοῦτο κελεύεις), where what is wanting to complete the sentence is involved in the words δοκοῦντ' ἐμοί.

1054. ἐξηύρομεν ζητοῦντες ἐχθίω Φρυγῶν, ὅστις. "We have clearly found him out on inquiry to be more hostile than the Phrygians." This refers to the deadly purpose against his confederates which Ajax had conceived when he went out by night to slay them. The following context, beginning with ὅστις, "being one who" &c., plainly shows this. The whole design of Ajax had been revealed by Athene, and by his own confessions.

ΣΟΦΟΚΛΕΟΥΣ

θανόντες ἂν προὐκείμεθ' αἰσχίστῳ μόρῳ,
οὗτος δ' ἂν ἔζη. νῦν δ' ἐνήλλαξεν θεὸς   1060
τὴν τοῦδ' ὕβριν πρὸς μῆλα καὶ ποίμνας πεσεῖν.
ὧν οὕνεκ' αὐτὸν οὔτις ἔστ' ἀνὴρ σθένων
τοσοῦτον ὥστε σῶμα τυμβεῦσαι τάφῳ,
ἀλλ' ἀμφὶ χλωρὰν ψάμαθον ἐκβεβλημένος
ὄρνισι φορβὴ παραλίοις γενήσεται.   1065
πρὸς ταῦτα μηδὲν δεινὸν ἐξάρῃς μένος.
εἰ γὰρ βλέποντος μὴ 'δυνήθημεν κρατεῖν
πάντως θανόντος γ' ἄρξομεν, κἂν μὴ θέλῃς,
χερσὶν παρευθύνοντες. οὐ γὰρ ἔσθ' ὅπου
λόγων ἀκοῦσαι ζῶν ποτ' ἠθέλησ' ἐμῶν.   1070
καίτοι κακοῦ πρὸς ἀνδρὸς ἄνδρα δημότην
μηδὲν δικαιοῦν τῶν ἐφεστώτων κλύειν.
οὐ γάρ ποτ' οὔτ' ἂν ἐν πόλει νόμοι καλῶς
φέροιντ' ἄν, ἔνθα μὴ καθεστήκῃ δέος,
οὔτ' ἂν στρατός γε σωφρόνως ἄρχοιτ' ἔτι   1075
μηδὲν φόβου πρόβλημα μηδ' αἰδοῦς ἔχων.
ἀλλ' ἄνδρα χρή, κἂν σῶμα γεννήσῃ μέγα,
δοκεῖν πεσεῖν ἂν κἂν ἀπὸ σμικροῦ κακοῦ.
δέος γὰρ ᾧ πρόσεστιν αἰσχύνη θ' ὁμοῦ,
σωτηρίαν ἔχοντα τόνδ' ἐπίστασο·   1080

1069. οὐ γὰρ ἔσθ' ὅπου, " for under no circumstances," or "in no possible way." See Matth. 402, obs. 2. Frequently when ἔστι is joined to a relative adverb or pronoun, the two together form a new indefinite adverb or pronoun.

1076. μηδὲν φόβου πρόβλημα. "Having no barrier or defence of fear and shame," that is, no barrier or defence, such as fear and a proper sense of shame would give to the army, against misrule and insubordination. Cf.

159, πύργου ῥῦμα. Moreover, that this was true of individuals also, as well as of corporate bodies, the speaker adds, v. 1079, δέος γὰρ ᾧ πρόσεστιν.

" When fear is blended with ingenuous shame,
The man, of both observant, is secure."—*Dale*.

Is secure, that is to say, against falling into any such misconduct as would bring upon him disgrace and punishment.

ΑΙΑΣ. 89

ὅπου δ' ὑβρίζειν δρᾶν θ' ἃ βούλεται παρῇ,
ταύτην νόμιζε τὴν πόλιν χρόνῳ ποτὲ
ἐξ οὐρίων δραμοῦσαν ἐς βυθὸν πεσεῖν.
ἀλλ' ἑστάτω μοι καὶ δέος τι καίριον,
καὶ μὴ δοκῶμεν δρῶντες ἃν ἡδώμεθα   1085
οὐκ ἀντιτίσειν αὖθις ἃν λυπώμεθα.
ἕρπει παραλλὰξ ταῦτα. πρόσθεν οὗτος ἦν
αἴθων ὑβριστής· νῦν δ' ἐγὼ μέγ' αὖ φρονῶ.
καί σοι προφωνῶ τόνδε μὴ θάπτειν, ὅπως
μὴ τόνδε θάπτων αὐτὸς ἐς ταφὰς πέσῃς.   1090

ΧΟΡΟΣ.
Μενέλαε, μὴ γνώμας ὑποστήσας σοφὰς
εἶτ' αὐτὸς ἐν θανοῦσιν ὑβριστὴς γένῃ.

ΤΕΥΚΡΟΣ.
οὐκ ἄν ποτ', ἄνδρες, ἄνδρα θαυμάσαιμ' ἔτι,
ὃς μηδὲν ὢν γοναῖσιν εἶθ' ἁμαρτάνει,
ὅθ' οἱ δοκοῦντες εὐγενεῖς πεφυκέναι   1095
τοιαῦθ' ἁμαρτάνουσιν ἐν λόγοις ἔπη.
ἄγ', εἴπ' ἀπ' ἀρχῆς αὖθις, ἢ σὺ φῂς ἄγειν
τὸν ἄνδρ' Ἀχαιοῖς δεῦρο σύμμαχον λαβών;
οὐκ αὐτὸς ἐξέπλευσεν, ὡς αὑτοῦ κρατῶν;
ποῦ σὺ στρατηγεῖς τοῦδε; ποῦ δὲ σοὶ λεῶν   1100
ἔξεστ' ἀνάσσειν ὧν ὅδ' ἡγεῖτ' οἴκοθεν;
Σπάρτης ἀνάσσων ἦλθες, οὐχ ἡμῶν κρατῶν.

1101. *ἡγεῖτ' οἴκοθεν.* All the MSS. *ἡγεῖτ'*, except one, which has *ἤγαγ'*. Porson conjectured *ἦγεν*; Elmsley *ἤγετ'*. *ἡγεῖτ'* is beyond all question the best word in itself, as being co-ordinate in its meaning with *ἀνάσσων*. It implies that Ajax led his men to the war as their independent *ἡγεμών*, and had quite as much authority to take the command (*ἡγεῖσθαι*) of them, as Menelaus had to rule (*ἀνάσσειν*) his own men from Sparta. The sole objection that has ever been alleged against the word *ἡγεῖτ'*, is one which respects the metre. That question is discussed in the Appendix.

οὐδ' ἔσθ' ὅπου σοὶ τόνδε κοσμῆσαι πλέον
ἀρχῆς ἔκειτο θεσμὸς ἢ καὶ τῷδε σέ.
ὕπαρχος ἄλλων δεῦρ' ἔπλευσας, οὐχ ὅλων   1105
στρατηγός, ὥστ' Αἴαντος ἡγεῖσθαί ποτε.
ἀλλ' ὧνπερ ἄρχεις ἄρχε, καὶ τὰ σέμν' ἔπη
κόλαζ' ἐκείνους· τόνδε δ', εἴτε μὴ σὺ φῇς
εἴθ' ἅτερος στρατηγός, ἐς ταφὰς ἐγὼ
θήσω δικαίως, οὐ τὸ σὸν δείσας στόμα.   1110
οὐ γάρ τι τῆς σῆς οὕνεκ' ἐστρατεύσατο
γυναικός, ὥσπερ οἱ πόνου πολλοῦ πλέῳ,
ἀλλ' οὕνεχ' ὅρκων οἷσιν ἦν ἐνώμοτος,
σοῦ δ' οὐδέν· οὐ γὰρ ἠξίου τοὺς μηδένας.
πρὸς ταῦτα πλείους δεῦρο κήρυκας λαβὼν   1115
καὶ τὸν στρατηγὸν ἧκε. τοῦ δὲ σοῦ ψόφου

1103, 1104. οὐδ' ἔσθ' ὅπου σοὶ .... ἢ καὶ τῷδε σέ. "Nor was there in any way a law of authority established, for you to rule him *any more than* (ἢ καὶ) for him to rule you." For a similar use of ἢ καὶ, cf. An. 927, εἰ δ' οἶδ' ἁμαρτάνουσι, μὴ πλείω κακὰ πάθοιεν ἢ καὶ δρῶσιν ἐκδίκως ἐμέ, and O. T. 93, τῶνδε γὰρ πλέον φέρω τὸ πένθος ἢ καὶ τῆς ἐμῆς πέρι; also cf. Hdt. 4. 118 and 5. 94; Xen. Cyr. 5. 5. 40.

1114. οὐ γὰρ ἠξίου τοὺς μηδένας. The v. ἀξιόω is seldom used to govern an accus. "He had no respect for worthless persons."— τοὺς μηδ., "nonentities," "good-for-nothing persons," an expression of great contempt.

1116. τοῦ δὲ σοῦ ψόφου οὐκ ἂν στραφείην. "But I will not be turned (that is, from my purpose) on account of your noise." L. and S. explain the genitive in the same manner: "C. gen. causae, τοῦ δὲ σοῦ ψόφου οὐκ ἂν στραφείην, ' I would not turn for any noise of thine.'" Menelaus was most imperious in forbidding the burial of Ajax, and Teucer was equally as determined not to be turned from it by all his clamorous threats. Cf. vv. 1109–1111. A very common way of translating it is, "I will not care for your noise;" and so Wunder: "significat στρέφεσθαι idem quod ἐντρέπεσθαι v. 90 positum."—ὡς ἂν ᾖς οἷός περ εἶ. Sophocles seems here to have gone quite out of the beaten track, in using ὡς for ἕως in this place, as well as in O. C. 1361, and Phil. 1330. Contrary though it be to all custom, yet it does not appear to be unintelligible. The preceding clause, in each of the three places where ὡς is used for ἕως, involves the notion of continuance for an indefinite length of time, and ὡς appears to compare it with a continuance for a length of time which is equally indefinite. Thus

ΑΙΑΣ. 91

οὐκ ἂν στραφείην, ὡς ἂν ᾖς οἷός περ εἶ.

ΧΟΡΟΣ.
οὐδ' αὖ τοιαύτην γλῶσσαν ἐν κακοῖς φιλῶ.
τὰ σκληρὰ γάρ τοι, κἂν ὑπέρδικ' ᾖ, δάκνει.

ΜΕΝΕΛΑΟΣ.
ὁ τοξότης ἔοικεν οὐ σμικρὸν φρονεῖν.   1120

ΤΕΥΚΡΟΣ.
οὐ γὰρ βάναυσον τὴν τέχνην ἐκτησάμην.

ΜΕΝΕΛΑΟΣ.
μέγ' ἄν τι κομπάσειας, ἀσπίδ' εἰ λάβοις.

ΤΕΥΚΡΟΣ.
κἂν ψιλὸς ἀρκέσαιμι σοί γ' ὡπλισμένῳ.

ΜΕΝΕΛΑΟΣ.
ἡ γλῶσσά σου τὸν θυμὸν ὡς δεινὸν τρέφει.

ΤΕΥΚΡΟΣ.
ξὺν τῷ δικαίῳ γὰρ μέγ' ἔξεστιν φρονεῖν.   1125

ΜΕΝΕΛΑΟΣ.
δίκαια γὰρ τόνδ' εὐτυχεῖν κτείναντά με;

ΤΕΥΚΡΟΣ.
κτείναντα; δεινόν γ' εἶπας, εἰ καὶ ζῇς θανών.

in Aj. 1117 the speaker says, "I will not be turned by reason of your clamour;" that is, "notwithstanding your clamour, I shall continue in my present purpose, *as* you continue to be such as you are." Here *as* is equivalent to *as long as*, for the comparison regards the length of time, and nothing else.

1126. κτείναντά με; "But is it right that a man who has killed me should fare well?" This is explained in 1128: "for a god preserves me, but with respect to this man, (as far as it lay in his power) I am no more." It is explained also in Hdt. I. 124, κατὰ μὲν γὰρ τὴν τούτου προθυμίην τέθνηκας· τὸ δὲ κατὰ θεούς τε καὶ ἐμὲ περίεις, and Xen. Cyr. 5. 4. 11, τὸ μὲν ἐπ' ἐμοὶ οἴχομαι, τὸ δ' ἐπὶ σοὶ σέσωσμαι.

ΣΟΦΟΚΛΕΟΥΣ

ΜΕΝΕΛΑΟΣ.
ὃς γὰρ ἐκσώζει με, τῷδε δ' οἴχομαι.
ΤΕΥΚΡΟΣ.
μή νυν ἀτίμα θεούς, θεοῖς σεσωσμένος.
ΜΕΝΕΛΑΟΣ.
ἐγὼ γὰρ ἂν ψέξαιμι δαιμόνων νόμους;   1130
ΤΕΥΚΡΟΣ.
εἰ τοὺς θανόντας οὐκ ἐᾷς θάπτειν παρών.
ΜΕΝΕΛΑΟΣ.
τούς γ' αὐτὸς αὐτοῦ πολεμίους. οὐ γὰρ καλόν.
ΤΕΥΚΡΟΣ.
ἦ σοὶ γὰρ Αἴας πολέμιος προὔστη ποτέ;
ΜΕΝΕΛΑΟΣ.
μισοῦντ' ἐμίσει· καὶ σὺ τοῦτ' ἠπίστασο.
ΤΕΥΚΡΟΣ.
κλέπτης γὰρ αὐτοῦ ψηφοποιὸς ηὑρέθης.   1135

1130. "But do you say that I should slight the laws of the gods?" He is indignant at the idea of it. Lobeck comp. Arist. Vesp. 1159, ἐγὼ γὰρ ἂν τλαίην; and Ar. Aves 815, Σπάρτην γὰρ ἂν θείμην ἐγώ;

1132. αὐτὸς αὐτοῦ πολ. "Of one at least who was a personal enemy to me I would not permit the burial, for it would not be becoming in me."—αὐτὸς αὐτοῦ seems to be a stronger expression than ἐμαυτοῦ. Cf. Eur. Heracl. 814, οὔτ' αὐτὸς αὐτοῦ δειλίαν (αἰδεσθείς). Menelaus seemed to think that personal enmity should override all other considerations, but the utterance of such a sentiment could never meet with the approval of a Greek assemblage with respect to the interment of a brave warrior. Such a sentiment, however, as coming from a Spartan king, might please the Athenians.

1135. κλέπτης γὰρ αὐτοῦ ψηφοποιὸς ηὑρέθης. "Thou wert discovered to be a fraudulent vote-maker against him."—αὐτοῦ is the objective genitive.—κλέπ. ψηφ. is, literally, "a vote-making cheat;" and the expression shows that a fraud had been committed in the forging of fictitious votes. Menelaus admits the fact when he says, "By the judges, and not by me, was he supplanted in this matter." It was they, he seems to say, who consciously accepted the fictitious votes. In Pind. N. 8. 45, κρυφίαισι γὰρ ἐν ψάφοις Ὀδυσσῆ Δαναοὶ θεράπευσαν, the expression κρυφ. ψάφ. could hardly mean real genuine votes obtained by undue influence, but rather the apocryphal or doubtful votes themselves that had been

ΑΙΑΣ. 93

ΜΕΝΕΛΑΟΣ.
ἐν τοῖς δικασταῖς, κοὐκ ἐμοὶ, τόδ᾽ ἐσφάλη.
ΤΕΥΚΡΟΣ.
πόλλ᾽ ἂν κακῶς λάθρα σὺ κλέψειας κακά.
ΜΕΝΕΛΑΟΣ.
τοῦτ᾽ εἰς ἀνίαν τοὔπος ἔρχεται τινί.
ΤΕΥΚΡΟΣ.
οὐ μᾶλλον, ὡς ἔοικεν, ἢ λυπήσομεν.
ΜΕΝΕΛΑΟΣ.
ἓν σοι φράσω· τόνδ᾽ ἐστὶν οὐχὶ θαπτέον.   1140
ΤΕΥΚΡΟΣ.
σὺ δ᾽ ἀντακούσει τοῦτον ὡς τεθάψεται.
ΜΕΝΕΛΑΟΣ.
ἤδη ποτ᾽ εἶδον ἄνδρ᾽ ἐγὼ γλώσσῃ θρασὺν
ναύτας ἐφορμήσαντα χειμῶνος τὸ πλεῖν,
ᾧ φθέγμ᾽ ἂν οὐκ ἂν ηὗρες, ἡνίκ᾽ ἐν κακῷ
χειμῶνος εἶχετ᾽, ἀλλ᾽ ὑφ᾽ εἵματος κρυφεὶς   1145
πατεῖν παρεῖχε τῷ θέλοντι ναυτίλων.
οὕτω δὲ καὶ σὲ καὶ τὸ σὸν λάβρον στόμα

secretly thrown into the urn, in order to swell the number in favour of Odysseus.
1138. τινί. τὶς is sometimes used for σὺ and ἐγὼ, as in v. 245, ὥρα τιν᾽: 413, ποῖ τις οὖν φύγοι; and v. 786, μὴ χαίρειν τινά Aristoph. Ran. 552, κακὸν ἥκει τινί: 554, δώσει τις δίκην: Ο. C. 1372, οὐ γὰρ ἔσθ᾽ ὅπως πόλιν | κείνην ἐρεῖ τις.
1142—1146. τὸ πλεῖν. "The infin. with the article is put for the infin. alone, because the infin. is considered as the subject or object of the main action." Matth. 542, obs. 2. Cf. Trach. 345, τὸ δ᾽ αὖ ξυνοικεῖν τῇδ᾽ ὁμοῦ τις ἂν γυνὴ δύναιτο;—χειμῶνος, a genitive of time, "in a time of storm," and it signifies here, "when a storm was beginning to arise." This simile, Lobeck has observed, has been imitated in part by other Greek writers, as Plat. Theaet. 191 A, ἐὰν δὲ πάντῃ ἀπορήσωμεν, ταπεινωθέντες, οἶμαι, τῷ λόγῳ παρέξομεν ὡς ναυτιῶντες πατεῖν τε καὶ χρῆσθαι ὅ τι ἂν βούληται, and Synesius, Epist. 4, μεθῆκεν ὁ κυβερνήτης τὸ πηδάλιον καὶ καταβαλὼν ἑαυτὸν πατεῖν παρεῖχε τῷ θέλοντι ναυτίλων.
1147. οὕτω δὲ καὶ σὲ κ.τ.λ. "In like manner a violent storm blowing from a little cloud" &c. The little cloud in the horizon is at first the only intimation that

σμικροῦ νέφους τάχ' ἄν τις ἐκπνεύσας μέγας
χειμὼν κατασβέσειε τὴν πολλὴν βοήν.

ΤΕΥΚΡΟΣ.

ἐγὼ δέ γ' ἄνδρ' ὄπωπα μωρίας πλέων,   1150
ὃς ἐν κακοῖς ὕβριζε τοῖσι τῶν πέλας·
κᾷτ' αὐτὸν εἰσιδών τις ἐμφερὴς ἐμοὶ
ὀργήν θ' ὅμοιος εἶπε τοιοῦτον λόγον,
ἄνθρωπε, μὴ δρᾶ τοὺς τεθνηκότας κακῶς·
εἰ γὰρ ποιήσεις, ἴσθι πημανούμενος.   1155
τοιαῦτ' ἄνολβον ἄνδρ' ἐνουθέτει παρών.
ὁρῶ δέ τοί νιν, κἄστιν, ὡς ἐμοὶ δοκεῖ,
οὐδείς ποτ' ἄλλος ἢ σύ. μῶν ᾐνιξάμην;

ΜΕΝΕΛΑΟΣ.

ἄπειμι· καὶ γὰρ αἰσχρὸν, εἰ πύθοιτό τις
λόγοις κολάζειν ᾧ βιάζεσθαι πάρα.   1160

ΤΕΥΚΡΟΣ.

ἄφερπέ νυν. κἀμοὶ γὰρ αἴσχιστον κλύειν
ἀνδρὸς ματαίου φλαῦρ' ἔπη μυθουμένου.

ΧΟΡΟΣ.

ἔσται μεγάλης ἔριδός τις ἀγών.
ἀλλ' ὡς δύνασαι, Τεῦκρε, ταχύνας
σπεῦσον κοίλην κάπετόν τιν' ἰδεῖν   1165
τῷδ', ἔνθα βροτοῖς τὸν ἀείμνηστον

a violent storm may be expected very shortly to come from that quarter. Thus the simile that goes before is perfect. The man who was so valorous in his talk when the storm was only beginning to arise, afterwards, when he was caught in the full fury of it, lay prostrate in fear, to be trodden upon at will by any of his fellow-sailors. There is a propensity sometimes shown in translating an ancient Greek poet to give a force to words which does not belong to them. ἐκπνεύσας is commonly translated "bursting forth," as if the first gust of wind that came to the ship from the little cloud was one of extreme violence. There is nothing, however, in the word itself to show that it was such, but only to show that it came from the little cloud.

ΑΙΑΣ.

τάφον εὐρώεντα καθέξει.

ΤΕΥΚΡΟΣ.

καὶ μὴν ἐς αὐτὸν καιρὸν οἵδε πλησίοι
πάρεισιν ἀνδρὸς τοῦδε παῖς τε καὶ γυνή,
τάφον περιστελοῦντε δυστήνου νεκροῦ. 1170
ὦ παῖ πρόσελθε δεῦρο, καὶ σταθεὶς πέλας
ἱκέτης ἔφαψαι πατρὸς, ὅς σ' ἐγείνατο.
θάκει δὲ προστρόπαιος ἐν χεροῖν ἔχων
κόμας ἐμὰς καὶ τῆσδε καὶ σαυτοῦ τρίτου,
ἱκτήριον θησαυρόν. εἰ δέ τις στρατοῦ 1175
βίᾳ σ' ἀποσπάσειε τοῦδε τοῦ νεκροῦ,
κακὸς κακῶς ἄθαπτος ἐκπέσοι χθονὸς,
γένους ἅπαντος ῥίζαν ἐξημημένος,
αὔτως ὅπωσπερ τόνδ' ἐγὼ τέμνω πλόκον.
ἔχ' αὐτὸν, ὦ παῖ, καὶ φύλασσε, μηδέ σε 1180
κινησάτω τις, ἀλλὰ προσπεσὼν ἔχου.
ὑμεῖς τε μὴ γυναῖκες ἀντ' ἀνδρῶν πέλας
παρέστατ', ἀλλ' ἀρήγετ', ἔς τ' ἐγὼ μόλω
τάφου μεληθεὶς τῷδε, κἂν μηδεὶς ἐᾷ.

ΧΟΡΟΣ.

τίς ἄρα νέατος ἐς πότε λήξει πολυπλάγκτων ἐτέων
ἀριθμὸς   στρ. α'. 1185
τὰν ἄπαυστον αἰὲν ἐμοὶ δορυσσόντων
μόχθων ἄταν ἐπάγων

1188. δορυσσόντων μόχθων. "That is ever bringing on me the unceasing woe of the toils of the spear." This can only be explained, in consistency with the description in vv. 600—608, on the supposition that the Chorus so far identified himself with the general army, as to say that he and his comrades suffered with it a life of unceasing toil, which the war had imposed on them. It is, however, to be observed, that in their continual night-watching in Mount Ida, they would have to go to it well armed. In Od. 14. 526 the swineherd goes armed to his night-watch, but how much more needful would this be in an enemy's country. The miseries of war which the Chorus afterwards gives a general

96 ΣΟΦΟΚΛΕΟΥΣ

ἀνὰ τὰν εὐρώδη Τροίαν, 1190
δύστανον ὄνειδος Ἑλλάνων;
ὄφελε πρότερον αἰθέρα δῦναι μέγαν ἢ τὸν πολύκοινον
 Ἅιδαν ἀντ. α΄. 1192
κεῖνος ἀνήρ, ὃς στυγερῶν ἔδειξεν ὅπλων 1195
Ἕλλασι κοινὸν Ἄρη.
ἰὼ πόνοι πρόπονοι.
κεῖνος γὰρ ἔπερσεν ἀνθρώπους.
ἐκεῖνος οὔτε στεφάνων στρ. β΄.
οὔτε βαθειᾶν κυλίκων 1200
νεῖμεν ἐμοὶ τέρψιν ὁμιλεῖν,
οὔτε γλυκὺν αὐλῶν ὄτοβον

description of in vv. 1200—1205, consisted entirely of a deprivation of home-pleasures, which a band of shepherds in a foreign country would suffer in an equal degree with the fighting-men. But there is one thing which the Chorus specially dwells upon, which was, his continual night-watching. This business to the rest of the army would only fall in succession each night on a small select number. It is also to be noticed that the Chorus says, that in their continual night-watching they lay on the dewy plain *uncared for—κεῖμαι δ' ἀμέριμνος οὕτως*. How could a part of the whole army complain of being uncared for, merely on account of their enduring the same amount of night-watching with all the rest of the army? but how exactly does this complaint suit the case of a band of shepherds removed far away out of sight, whose hard life and unceasing toils by night were little thought of and scarcely understood by the rest of the army. Moreover, when the Chorus speaks of the loss which he had sustained in Ajax his former protector, he speaks of him only as his protector from the fears and darts of the night; but not one word does he say of his having been a bulwark to him, as he was to the rest of the army, against his foes in the daytime in the open field of battle.

1190, 1191. ἀνὰ τὰν εὐρώδη Τροίαν. "Throughout the wide land of Troia, a name of sad reproach to the Hellenes."—δύστ. ὄνειδος is put in apposition to Τροίαν. The Chorus, so far from entertaining the hope of returning home laden with the spoils of victory, now rather believes that the siege of Troy will prove an utter failure, and that the very name of that land will be a reproach to its invaders. It is the opinion of most critics that εὐρώδης in this place is derived from εὐρύς, in the same manner as from βραχὺς and τραχὺς come βραχώδης and τραχώδης. The question of metre in v. 1190 and v. 1188 is discussed in the Appendix.

ΑΙΑΣ.

δύσμορος οὔτ' ἐννυχίαν
τέρψιν ἰαύειν ἐρώτων·
ἐρώτων δ' ἀπέπαυσεν, ὤμοι.   1205
κεῖμαι δ' ἀμέριμνος οὕτως,
ἀεὶ πυκιναῖς δρόσοις
τεγγόμενος κόμας,
λυγρᾶς μνήματα Τροίας.   1210
καὶ πρὶν μὲν ἐννυχίου   ἀντ. β'.
δείματος ἦν μοι προβολὰ
καὶ βελέων θούριος Αἴας,
νῦν δ' οὗτος ἀνεῖται στυγερῷ
δαίμονι. τίς μοι, τίς ἔτ' οὖν   1215
τέρψις ἐπέσται;
γενοίμαν ἵν' ὑλᾶεν ἔπεστι πόντου
πρόβλημ' ἁλίκλυστον, ἄκραν
ὑπὸ πλάκα Σουνίου,   1220
τὰς ἱερὰς ὅπως
προσείποιμεν Ἀθάνας.

ΤΕΥΚΡΟΣ.

καὶ μὴν ἰδὼν ἔσπευσα τὸν στρατηλάτην
Ἀγαμέμνον' ἡμῖν δεῦρο τόνδ' ὁρμώμενον
δῆλος δέ μοὐστὶ σκαιὸν ἐκλύσων στόμα.   1225

ΑΓΑΜΕΜΝΩΝ.

σὲ δὴ τὰ δεινὰ ῥήματ' ἀγγέλλουσί μοι

1214. στυγερῷ δαίμονι. Wunder thinks that it cannot be doubted that στυγερὸς δαίμων means Pluto. Musgrave leans to the same opinion. Indeed, it is difficult to imagine to whom the epithet στυγερὸς could be so fitly applied as to him who was said to preside over the abhorred region of the dead: τὸν ἀπότροπον ἀΐδηλον Ἀΐδαν, 608. "But this man has been devoted to the loathed daemon" of death.

1221. τὰς ἱερὰς ὅπως. It was the custom, it is said, for mariners on coming within the first sight of the land to which they were sailing, to hail it with loud shoutings of joy. "Italiam laeto socii clamore salutant," Aen. 3. 524. It appears that the helmet of Minerva on the Acropolis was discernible from the promontory of Sunium.

ΣΟΦΟΚΛΕΟΥΣ

τλῆναι καθ' ἡμῶν ὧδ' ἀνοιμωκτὶ χανεῖν;
σέ τοι, τὸν ἐκ τῆς αἰχμαλωτίδος λέγω,
ἦ που τραφεὶς ἂν μητρὸς εὐγενοῦς ἄπο
ὑψήλ' ἐκόμπεις κἀπ' ἄκρων ὡδοιπόρεις,   1230
ὅτ' οὐδὲν ὢν τοῦ μηδὲν ἀντέστης ὕπερ,
κοὔτε στρατηγοὺς οὔτε ναυάρχους μολεῖν
ἡμᾶς Ἀχαιῶν οὔτε σοῦ διωμόσω·
ἀλλ' αὐτὸς ἄρχων, ὡς σὺ φῇς, Αἴας ἔπλει.
ταῦτ' οὐκ ἀκούειν μεγάλα πρὸς δούλων κακά;   1235
ποίου κέκραγας ἀνδρὸς ὧδ' ὑπέρφρονα;
ποῖ βάντος ἢ ποῦ στάντος οὗπερ οὐκ ἐγώ;
οὐκ ἄρ' Ἀχαιοῖς ἄνδρες εἰσὶ πλὴν ὅδε;
πικροὺς ἔοιγμεν τῶν Ἀχιλλείων ὅπλων
ἀγῶνας Ἀργείοισι κηρῦξαι τότε,   1240
εἰ πανταχοῦ φανούμεθ' ἐκ Τεύκρου κακοὶ,
κοὐκ ἀρκέσει ποθ' ὑμῖν οὐδ' ἡσσημένοις
εἴκειν ἃ τοῖς πολλοῖσιν ἤρεσκεν κριταῖς,
ἀλλ' αἰὲν ἡμᾶς ἢ κακοῖς βαλεῖτέ που
ἢ σὺν δόλῳ κεντήσεθ' οἱ λελειμμένοι.   1245
ἐκ τῶνδε μέντοι τῶν τρόπων οὐκ ἄν ποτε
κατάστασις γένοιτ' ἂν οὐδενὸς νόμου,
εἰ τοὺς δίκῃ νικῶντας ἐξωθήσομεν
καὶ τοὺς ὄπισθεν ἐς τὸ πρόσθεν ἄξομεν.
ἀλλ' εἰρκτέον τάδ' ἐστίν. οὐ γὰρ οἱ πλατεῖς   1250

1231. ὅτ' οὐδὲν ὢν τοῦ μηδὲν ἀντέστης ὕπερ. "When being nothing yourself, you stand up for one who is as nothing." The change from οὐδὲν to μηδὲν intimates that there is a change in the sense. Whereas οὐδὲν is here used as an expression of contempt for the object of it, μηδὲν simply signifies that the object of it was brought to nothing by death. It is in the sense of a person being brought to nothing by death, or brought to extreme misery, or doomed to death, that οὐδὲν as well as μηδὲν is generally used when applied to a person, as in Elect. 1166, τὴν μηδὲν ἐς τὸ μηδέν, and Eur. Andr. 1077, οὐδέν εἰμ'· ἀπωλόμην. On the other hand, in Aj. 1114 τοὺς μηδένας in the plural is an expression of contempt.

ΑΙΑΣ.   99

οὐδ' εὐρύνωτοι φῶτες ἀσφαλέστατοι,
ἀλλ' οἱ φρονοῦντες εὖ κρατοῦσι πανταχοῦ.
μέγας δὲ πλευρὰ βοῦς ὑπὸ σμικρᾶς ὅμως
μάστιγος ὀρθὸς εἰς ὁδὸν πορεύεται.
καὶ σοὶ προσέρπον τοῦτ' ἐγὼ τὸ φάρμακον   1255
ὁρῶ τάχ', εἰ μὴ νοῦν κατακτήσει τινά·
ὃς ἀνδρὸς οὐκέτ' ὄντος, ἀλλ' ἤδη σκιᾶς,
θαρσῶν ὑβρίζεις κἀξελευθεροστομεῖς.
οὐ σωφρονήσεις; οὐ μαθὼν ὃς εἶ φύσιν
ἄλλον τιν' ἄξεις ἄνδρα δεῦρ' ἐλεύθερον,   1260
ὅστις πρὸς ἡμᾶς ἀντὶ σοῦ λέξει τὰ σά;
σοῦ γὰρ λέγοντος οὐκέτ' ἂν μάθοιμ' ἐγώ·
τὴν βάρβαρον γὰρ γλῶσσαν οὐκ ἐπαΐω.

ΧΟΡΟΣ.
εἴθ' ὑμῖν ἀμφοῖν νοῦς γένοιτο σωφρονεῖν.
τούτου γὰρ οὐδὲν σφῷν ἔχω λῷον φράσαι.   1265

ΤΕΥΚΡΟΣ.
φεῦ· τοῦ θανόντος ὡς ταχεῖά τις βροτοῖς

1252. οἱ φρονοῦντες εὖ. The position of εὖ after the verb makes it more emphatic. Cf. 371, φρόνησον εὖ; An. 166, 410, and 723; and O. T. 308. In O. C. 1497 παθὼν stands alone, which is admitted to be a most unusual circumstance when it is taken in a good sense. There, however, there is a gap in the line which requires to be filled up exactly in that part of it, which makes it probable that παθὼν was followed with εὖ; for it must be allowed by all, I think, that a hearty and emphatic expression of thankfulness for the kind treatment he had received would in that place have come well from the speaker.

1266. φεῦ· τοῦ θανόντος ὡς ταχεῖά τις. Here τις is joined to the predicate ταχεῖα, and must not be taken with χάρις; but inasmuch as ταχὺς, when it is joined to a verb, is usually construed as an adverb, it is not easy in a translation to express the meaning of τις, except in some such way as follows: "Alas! how among mankind is all favour for one that is dead *a quick* thing to fade away." Thus in O. C. 307 δεῦρ' ἀφίξεται ταχὺς does not mean he will come with a quick step, but he will be quick to come, that is, he will not delay his coming—as if the idiomatic phrase were ταχύς ἔσται ἀφικνεῖσθαι. In like manner I

100   ΣΟΦΟΚΛΕΟΥΣ

χάρις διαρρεῖ καὶ προδοῦσ' ἁλίσκεται,
εἰ σοῦ γ' ὅδ' ἀνὴρ οὐδ' ἐπὶ σμικρῶν λόγων,
Αἴας, ἔτ' ἴσχει μνῆστιν, οὗ σὺ πολλάκις
τὴν σὴν προτείνων προὔκαμες ψυχὴν δόρει·   1270
ἀλλ' οἴχεται δὴ πάντα ταῦτ' ἐρριμμένα.
ὦ πολλὰ λέξας ἄρτι κἀνόνητ' ἔπη,
οὐ μνημονεύεις οὐκέτ' οὐδέν, ἡνίκα
ἑρκέων ποθ' ὑμᾶς οὗτος ἐγκεκλειμένους,
ἤδη τὸ μηδὲν ὄντας, ἐν τροπῇ δορὸς   1275

think that ὡς ταχεῖά τις χάρις διαρρεῖ is the same as if the idiomatic phrase were ὡς χάρις τις ταχεῖα (sc. χάρις) ἐστι διαρρεῖν. Cf. An. 951, ἀλλ' ἁ μοιριδία τις δύνασις δεινά, " but the power of fate is *a terrible* power." The above explanation of τις ταχεῖα may not in all points be the correct one; but however it may be better explained, of one thing I am quite sure, and that is, that ταχεῖα being joined with τις, is not used as an adverb, but is used as an adjective agreeing with χάρις; and that, quite as much as in the passage above quoted from the An. of Soph., δεινά is an adjective agreeing with δύνασις.

1268. οὐδ' ἐπὶ σμικρῶν λόγων. " Not even on small accounts." The thing which was the subject of their present consideration was the burial of Ajax, which ought to have been a matter of small account for Agamemnon to concede in favour of one who had rendered him such important services in the field of battle.

1274. ἑρκέων . . . . ἐγκεκλειμένους. In Il. 12. 33—39 the Grecians had been driven back, and were shut up within their intrenchments (ἑρκέων ἐγ.). At the end of Il. 14 and beginning of Il. 15, Hector having been almost wounded to death with a great stone which Ajax had hurled against him, the Grecians are set free, and renew the battle in the open plain, until at length they are again put to flight, and are a second time shut up within their intrenchments.

" And if any Trojan came
Obsequious to the will of Hector,
    armed
With fire to burn the fleet, on
    his spear's point
Ajax receiving wounded him,
    until
Twelve died in conflict with
    himself alone."—*Cowper*.

At length Hector with his great sword lops off the brazen point of the ashen javelin of Ajax, who being now worn out with fatigue retires from the fight. The Trojans then set fire to the ship. Achilles, seeing the flames from his tent, sends Patroclus clad in his own arms. The Trojans are affrighted, thinking that it is Achilles himself. Patroclus drives them out, and quenches the fire. The final victory, therefore, was due to Patroclus.

ΑΙΑΣ. 101

ἐρρύσατ' ἐλθὼν μοῦνος, ἀμφὶ μὲν νεῶν
ἄκροισιν ἤδη ναυτικοῖς ἐδωλίοις
πυρὸς φλέγοντος, ἐς δὲ ναυτικὰ σκάφη
πηδῶντος ἄρδην Ἕκτορος τάφρων ὕπερ;
τίς ταῦτ' ἀπεῖρξεν; οὐχ ὅδ' ἦν ὁ δρῶν τάδε,   1280
ὃν οὐδαμοῦ φῂς οὐδὲ συμβῆναι ποδί;
ἆρ' ὑμὶν οὗτος ταῦτ' ἔδρασεν ἔνδικα;
χὤτ' αὖθις αὐτὸς Ἕκτορος μόνος μόνου,
λαχών τε κἀκέλευστος, ἦλθ' ἐναντίος,
οὐ δραπέτην τὸν κλῆρον ἐς μέσον καθεὶς,   1285
ὑγρᾶς ἀρούρας βῶλον, ἀλλ' ὃς εὐλόφου
κυνῆς ἔμελλε πρῶτος ἅλμα κουφιεῖν;
ὅδ' ἦν ὁ πράσσων ταῦτα, σὺν δ' ἐγὼ παρών,
ὁ δοῦλος, οὐκ τῆς βαρβάρου μητρὸς γεγώς.

1283. χὤτ' αὖθις αὐτὸς Ἕκτορος μόνος μόνου κ.τ.λ. According to Apollodorus, the vessel into which the chiefs cast their lots for the division of Peloponnesus among the Heraclidae was a water-pot filled with water; and as it was determined that Messenia should become the possession of him whose lot came out last, while the others threw in pebbles, Chresphontes, who wished to procure Messenia, threw in a ball of earth which melted in the water, and by this artifice he obtained his wish. Sophocles in alluding to this story accommodates it to the case of lots thrown into a dry helmet, by supposing that one of the lots might be a ball of earth that was saturated with water beforehand. In Il. 7 this single combat takes up a great part of the book. Ajax with eight other distinguished warriors accepted Hector's challenge. It appears that each of the warriors inscribed his own private mark on his lot, and as soon as all the lots had been thrown into the helmet of Agamemnon, the people lifted up their hands in prayer to the gods that the lot might fall on Ajax more than any other; and according to the will of the gods, 7. 182, ὃν ἄρ' ἤθελον αὐτοί, the lot of Ajax sprang out first; and when it had been carried round, Ajax recognizes his own mark and rejoices, Il. 7. 189. When the single combat had been continued on till night, the heralds Talthybius and Idaeus stretched out their sceptres between them, and parted them, upon which occasion they exchanged gifts—

" that Greek alike
And Trojan, speaking of our
  strife may say,
Furious they met; with soul-
  consuming rage
Assailed each other—but they
  parted friends."—*Cowper*.

102 ΣΟΦΟΚΛΕΟΥΣ

δύστηνε, ποῖ βλέπων ποτ' αὐτὰ καὶ θροεῖς; 1290
οὐκ οἶσθα σοῦ πατρὸς μὲν ὃς προὔφυ πατὴρ
ἀρχαῖον ὄντα Πέλοπα βάρβαρον Φρύγα;
'Ατρέα δ', ὃς αὖ σ' ἔσπειρε δυσσεβέστατον
προθέντ' ἀδελφῷ δεῖπνον οἰκείων τέκνων;
αὐτὸς δὲ μητρὸς ἐξέφυς Κρήσσης, ἐφ' ᾗ 1295
λαβὼν ἐπακτὸν ἄνδρ' ὁ φιτύσας πατὴρ

1293. Ἀτρέα δ', ὃς αὖ σ' ἔσπειρε δυσσεβέστατον κ.τ.λ. I have written this sentence without putting any comma either before or after the word δυσσεβέστατον, because there is a great diversity of opinion as to which of three objects it ought to be applied. Some apply it to Ἀτρέα, some to σ', and others again to δεῖπνον. In a case of this kind one way of testing the truth is the manner in which the sentence may most easily and effectively be spoken in the Greek original. If δυσσεβέστατον be spoken in such a tone as if the speaker were still about to mention the thing to which he meant to apply it, the attention of the hearers would be held in a suspended expectation of hearing what it was, for they would instantly understand that the thing had not been mentioned. On the other hand, it would be much more difficult to speak the sentence in such a manner as to make the hearers clearly understand that this epithet belonged to σ', and not to Ἀτρέα, or to Ἀτρέα and not to σ'. In the *Quarterly Review*, No. 7, p. 799, Elmsley expunges the comma after δυσσεβέστατον, that it may agree with δεῖπνον.—The method that has been adopted in this note of testing the truth of what appears to be the correct translation of the passage, may, I think, be applied with good effect to that passage in O.T. 328, which has so much exercised the minds of critics; for if in the speaking of the words ἐγὼ δ' οὐ μή ποτε, τἄμ' ὡς ἂν εἴπω μὴ, τὰ σ' ἐκφήνω κακά, a due emphasis be laid on τἄμ' and on τὰ σ', as opposed to each other, and a proper pause be observed after ποτε, and again after the second μὴ, the meaning of the whole sentence will at once become clear, which is this: "I will never reveal your misfortunes, that I may avoid the mention of my own." τἄμ' ὡς ἂν εἴπω μὴ, being taken together thus, form the subordinate member of the sentence, dividing the principal one into two parts, and nothing more is required to show this in the speaking of it, than a pause being observed at the beginning and end of it.

1295, 1296. αὐτὸς δὲ μητρὸς ἐξέφυς .... ὁ φιτύσας πατήρ. The expression μητρὸς ἐξέφυς seems likely to have suggested its kindred one in the following line, ὁ φιτύσας πατήρ, and this makes it hardly conceivable that they were not intended to express the same parental relationship to Agamemnon. Thus also the dramatic effect is heightened, for

ἐφῆκεν ἐλλοῖς ἰχθύσιν διαφθοράν.
τοιοῦτος ὢν τοιῷδ' ὀνειδίζεις σποράν;
ὃς ἐκ πατρὸς μέν εἰμι Τελαμῶνος γεγώς,
ὅστις στρατοῦ τὰ πρῶτ' ἀριστεύσας ἐμὴν   1300
ἴσχει ξύνευνον μητέρ', ἣ φύσει μὲν ἦν
βασίλεια, Λαομέδοντος· ἔκκριτον δέ νιν
δώρημ' ἐκείνῳ 'δωκεν Ἀλκμήνης γόνος.
ἆρ' ὧδ' ἄριστος ἐξ ἀριστέοιν δυοῖν
βλαστὼν ἂν αἰσχύνοιμι τοὺς πρὸς αἵματος,   1305
οὓς νῦν σὺ τοιοῖσδ' ἐν πόνοισι κειμένους
ὠθεῖς ἀθάπτους, οὐδ' ἐπαισχύνει λέγων;
εὖ νυν τόδ' ἴσθι, τοῦτον εἰ βαλεῖτέ που,
βαλεῖτε χἠμᾶς τρεῖς ὁμοῦ συγκειμένους.
ἐπεὶ καλόν μοι τοῦδ' ὑπερπονουμένῳ   1310
θανεῖν προδήλως μᾶλλον ἢ τῆς σῆς ὑπὲρ
γυναικός, ἢ τοῦ σοῦ θ' ὁμαίμονος λέγω;

we may then imagine the speaker, by the very manner in which he utters the words ὁ φιτύσας πατήρ, to intimate to Agamemnon the lasting infamy which his own father had bequeathed to him by the ignominious death to which he had doomed his mother. But however much opinions might have differed on this point, if there had been nothing else to fix the meaning of the words ὁ φιτύσας πατήρ, the words which follow ought to have set that matter at rest : for how could the father of Agamemnon's mother have cast her into the sea to be a prey to the dumb fishes, if she lived afterwards to be married to Atreus? The critics who cleave to the idea that ὁ φιτύσας πατήρ must mean the father of Agamemnon's mother, are obliged to force upon the word ἐφῆκεν a meaning which is quite foreign to it, to say nothing about the expression ἐπακτὸν ἄνδρα. Among those critics, however, Dindorf concludes his note on the subject with the following candid admission :—" We must confess that the words ἐπακτὸν ἄνδρα are more fitly spoken of Thyestes than of a slave of Catreus; and that the words ἐφῆκεν ἐλλοῖς ἰχθύσιν διαφθορὰν seem rather to say that Aerope perished in the sea than that she was preserved from such a death by the deceit of Nauplius." There ought not to be a doubt about the matter.

1312. ἢ τοῦ σοῦ θ' ὁμαίμονος λέγω. There is something faulty in this ending of the sentence. Of all the various explanations which have been put forth of λέγω, not one is so satisfactory as to commend itself

104   ΣΟΦΟΚΛΕΟΤΣ

πρὸς ταῦθ' ὅρα μὴ τοὐμὸν, ἀλλὰ καὶ τὸ σόν.
ὡς εἴ με πημανεῖς τι, βουλήσει ποτὲ
καὶ δειλὸς εἶναι μᾶλλον ἢ 'ν ἐμοὶ θρασύς.   1315
ΧΟΡΟΣ.
ἄναξ Ὀδυσσεῦ, καιρὸν ἴσθ' ἐληλυθὼς,
εἰ μὴ ξυνάψων, ἀλλὰ συλλύσων πάρει.
ΟΔΥΣΣΕΥΣ.
τί δ' ἔστιν, ἄνδρες; τηλόθεν γὰρ ᾐσθόμην
βοὴν Ἀτρειδῶν τῷδ' ἐπ' ἀλκίμῳ νεκρῷ.
ΑΓΑΜΕΜΝΩΝ.
οὐ γὰρ κλύοντές ἐσμεν αἰσχίστους λόγους,   1320
ἄναξ Ὀδυσσεῦ, τοῦδ' ὑπ' ἀνδρὸς ἀρτίως;

to anything like a general acceptance, nor is it defended by the bringing forward of anything like a similar use or position of it in any other sentence. The particle θ' is also equally indefensible. Dindorf's correction of it is τοῦ σοῦ ξυναίμονος; Herm., τοῦ σοῦ γ'; and Donaldson, τοῦ τοῦδ'; for he supposes Menelaus to be present; but it does not appear that the dem. pron. ὅδε, when used of a person present, has ever the article prefixed to it; and with respect to σοῦ γ', it does not appear that the poss. pron. σὸς has ever the particle γὲ suffixed to it. The same appears to be the case with the poss. pron. ἐμός. This, if it be really a fact, is a very remarkable one, however it may be accounted for. The conclusion to which it leads us is inevitable, that τοῦ σοῦ γ' is not the sort of Greek which Sophocles would have used.

1316. καιρὸν is a briefer expression for ἐς καιρὸν, as in v. 34.—ἴσθ' ἐληλυθώς. It appears to be a general rule of Greek syntax that the participle should be in the same case with the subject of the finite verb, when the subject of both is the same. Cf. 1155, ἴσθι πημανούμενος. 471, δηλώσω . . . γεγώς. 807, ἔγνωκα . . . ἠπατημένη. There are some exceptions, as for instance when the subject, being a person, takes a reflexive view of himself. Trach. 706, ὁρῶ δέ μ' ἔργον δεινὸν ἐξειργασμένην.

1317. εἰ πάρει κ.τ.λ. "If you are come not to fasten but to loosen," that is, if you are come not to aggravate the strife, but to allay it. Cf. An. 40, λύουσ' ἂν ἢ 'φάπτουσα. It seems to be a proverbial expression which might be applied to any entanglement where care was required, lest in your endeavours to loose it, you should draw it tighter together.

ΑΙΑΣ. 105

ΟΔΥΣΣΕΥΣ.
ποίους ; ἐγὼ γὰρ ἀνδρὶ συγγνώμην ἔχω
κλύοντι φλαῦρα συμβαλεῖν ἔπη κακά.
ΑΓΑΜΕΜΝΩΝ.
ἤκουσεν αἰσχρά· δρῶν γὰρ ἦν τοιαῦτά με.
ΟΔΥΣΣΕΥΣ.
τί γάρ σ᾽ ἔδρασεν, ὥστε καὶ βλάβην ἔχειν ;   1325
ΑΓΑΜΕΜΝΩΝ.
οὔ φησ᾽ ἐάσειν τόνδε τὸν νεκρὸν ταφῆς
ἄμοιρον, ἀλλὰ πρὸς βίαν θάψειν ἐμοῦ.
ΟΔΥΣΣΕΥΣ.
ἔξεστιν οὖν εἰπόντι τἀληθῆ φίλῳ
σοὶ μηδὲν ἧσσον ἢ πάρος ξυνηρετμεῖν ;
ΑΓΑΜΕΜΝΩΝ.
εἴπ᾽· ἦ γὰρ εἴην οὐκ ἂν εὖ φρονῶν, ἐπεὶ   1330
φίλον σ᾽ ἐγὼ μέγιστον Ἀργείων νέμω.
ΟΔΥΣΣΕΥΣ.
ἄκουέ νυν.   τὸν ἄνδρα τόνδε πρὸς θεῶν
μὴ τλῇς ἄθαπτον ὧδ᾽ ἀναλγήτως βαλεῖν·
μηδ᾽ ἡ βία σε μηδαμῶς νικησάτω

1334. μηδ᾽ ἡ βία. This word is supposed by some critics to mean in this place *extreme violence of temper*. "Nor let ungoverned *wrath* Subdue thy calmer mood." Dale. Instead of referring to any feeling of the mind, it seems rather simply to express the abstract notion of *might* or *power*, or when might or power is put into wrongful action, the notion of *violence*, or *an act of violence*. On the present occasion it refers to the might of Agamemnon's authority. Odysseus had asked him whether Teucer had done him any injury, in answer to which question all that Agamemnon had to allege against him was, that he had the audacity to say that he would bury the body of Ajax *in defiance of his authority* (πρὸς βίαν . . . ἐμοῦ). Upon this Odysseus admonishes Agamemnon not to use his authority (μηδ᾽ ἡ βία) in a wrongful manner.

"Then hear me, by the gods
  I must entreat thee.
Do not remorseless and in-
  human cast
The body forth unburied, nor
  permit
Authority to trample thus
  on justice."—*Francklin.*

τοσόνδε μισεῖν ὥστε τὴν δίκην πατεῖν. 1335
κἀμοὶ γὰρ ἦν ποθ᾽ οὗτος ἔχθιστος στρατοῦ,
ἐξ οὗ 'κράτησα τῶν Ἀχιλλείων ὅπλων·
ἀλλ᾽ αὐτὸν ἔμπας ὄντ᾽ ἐγὼ τοιόνδ᾽ ἐμοὶ
οὐκ ἂν ἀτιμάσαιμ᾽ ἄν, ὥστε μὴ λέγειν
ἕν᾽ ἄνδρ᾽ ἰδεῖν ἄριστον Ἀργείων, ὅσοι 1340
Τροίαν ἀφικόμεσθα, πλὴν Ἀχιλλέως.
ὥστ᾽ οὐκ ἂν ἐνδίκως γ᾽ ἀτιμάζοιτό σοι.
οὐ γάρ τι τοῦτον, ἀλλὰ τοὺς θεῶν νόμους
φθείροις ἄν. ἄνδρα δ᾽ οὐ δίκαιον, εἰ θάνοι,
βλάπτειν τὸν ἐσθλόν, οὐδ᾽ ἐὰν μισῶν κυρῇς. 1345

ΑΓΑΜΕΜΝΩΝ.

σὺ ταῦτ᾽, Ὀδυσσεῦ, τοῦδ᾽ ὑπερμαχεῖς ἐμοί;

ΟΔΥΣΣΕΥΣ.

ἔγωγ᾽· ἐμίσουν δ᾽, ἡνίκ᾽ ἦν μισεῖν καλόν.

ΑΓΑΜΕΜΝΩΝ.

οὐ γὰρ θανόντι καὶ προσεμβῆναί σε χρή;

ΟΔΥΣΣΕΥΣ.

μὴ χαῖρ᾽, Ἀτρείδη, κέρδεσιν τοῖς μὴ καλοῖς.

ΑΓΑΜΕΜΝΩΝ.

τόν τοι τύραννον εὐσεβεῖν οὐ ῥᾴδιον. 1350

The Schol. μὴ ἡ ἐξουσία βιασάσθω σε, ὥστε πρᾶξαί τι παρὰ τὸ δίκαιον· τουτέστι μὴ ὑπὲρ τοῦ ἐνδείξασθαι τούτῳ τὴν ἐξουσίαν παραβῇς τὸ δίκαιον.

1339. οὐκ ἄν. This reading can hardly be right, for it does not appear that ἄν can be made long. The correction which is most generally approved, and bears in it the greatest probability of being the right one, is that which was proposed by ▓▓▓▓, that is, οὗτοι ἄν.

1350. τόν τοι τύραννον εὐσεβεῖν οὐ ῥᾴδιον. "It is not easy for the supreme ruler to be religious." This general observation is here made with a special reference to the burial of Ajax. It was intended to be a reply to what Odysseus had just said, namely, that it was a duty of religion, or of reverence towards the gods, as well as of justice to so great a warrior as Ajax had been, to permit his body to be buried. In his answer to this

ΑΙΑΣ.

ΟΔΥΣΣΕΥΣ.
ἀλλ' εὖ λέγουσι τοῖς φίλοις τιμὰς νέμειν.
ΑΓΑΜΕΜΝΩΝ.
κλύειν τὸν ἐσθλὸν ἄνδρα χρὴ τῶν ἐν τέλει.
ΟΔΥΣΣΕΥΣ.
παῦσαι· κρατεῖς τοι τῶν φίλων νικώμενος.
ΑΓΑΜΕΜΝΩΝ.
μέμνησ' ὁποίῳ φωτὶ τὴν χάριν δίδως.
ΟΔΥΣΣΕΥΣ.
ὅδ' ἐχθρὸς ἀνὴρ, ἀλλὰ γενναῖός ποτ' ἦν.   1355
ΑΓΑΜΕΜΝΩΝ.
τί ποτε ποιήσεις; ἐχθρὸν ὧδ' αἰδεῖ νέκυν;
ΟΔΥΣΣΕΥΣ.
νικᾷ γὰρ ἀρετή με τῆς ἔχθρας πολύ.
ΑΓΑΜΕΜΝΩΝ.
τοιοίδε μέντοι φῶτες ἔμπληκτοι βροτῶν.

Agamemnon acknowledges the truth of the religious principle, and he does not controvert the justice of the case, but he puts forward a poor excuse for not acting upon it. It was not easy for one in his high position as the king to do so. The difficulty which stood in his way he afterwards explains in v. 1362. He was afraid that he would be looked upon by the people as a coward, if he did not revenge himself on his enemy by forbidding his burial. He thought it therefore good policy to pay more regard to the opinion of the people than to the principles of piety and justice. It surely could not be very wrong in him, he thought, as the supreme ruler, to uphold the dignity of his throne in the opinion of the people whom he governed, even though by so doing he should disregard the principles of piety and justice. Cf. An. 743—745, Ai. οὐ γὰρ δίκαιά σ' ἐξαμαρτάνονθ' ὁρῶ. Κρ. ἁμαρτάνω γὰρ τὰς ἐμὰς ἀρχὰς σέβων; Ai. οὐ γὰρ σέβεις, τιμάς γε τὰς θεῶν πατῶν.

1358. τοιοίδε μέντοι φῶτες ἔμπληκτοι βροτῶν. Odysseus having said that the worth of Ajax as a brave warrior had with him more than counterbalanced any feeling of personal enmity, Agamemnon replies, "Yet such men as he are unstable;" that is to say, those who carry their enmity to such an excess as he has done, are not steadied by any fixed principles of action. They are driven about by the impulse of their own passions. There is no sta-

108 ΣΟΦΟΚΛΕΟΤΣ

ΟΔΥΣΣΕΥΣ.
ἦ κάρτα πολλοὶ νῦν φίλοι καὖθις πικροί.
ΑΓΑΜΕΜΝΩΝ.
τοιούσδ᾽ ἐπαινεῖς δῆτα σὺ κτᾶσθαι φίλους;   1360
ΟΔΥΣΣΕΥΣ.
σκληρὰν ἐπαινεῖν οὐ φιλῶ ψυχὴν ἐγώ.
ΑΓΑΜΕΜΝΩΝ.
ἡμᾶς σὺ δειλοὺς τῇδε θἠμέρᾳ φανεῖς.
ΟΔΥΣΣΕΥΣ.
ἄνδρας μὲν οὖν Ἕλλησι πᾶσιν ἐνδίκους.
ΑΓΑΜΕΜΝΩΝ.
ἄνωγας οὖν με τὸν νεκρὸν θάπτειν ἐᾶν;
ΟΔΥΣΣΕΥΣ.
ἔγωγε. καὶ γὰρ αὐτὸς ἐνθάδ᾽ ἵξομαι.   1365
ΑΓΑΜΕΜΝΩΝ.
ἦ πάνθ᾽ ὅμοια πᾶς ἀνὴρ αὑτῷ πονεῖ.

bility in them, so that any one might place any dependence upon them. They are inconsistent with themselves, and inconstant to others. See Plat. Lysis. 214 c, μηδέποθ᾽ ὁμοίους μηδ᾽ αὐτοὺς αὐτοῖς εἶναι, ἀλλ᾽ ἐμπλήκτους τε καὶ ἀσταθμήτους. Odysseus could not deny what had been said, and simply replies that many others from being friends have become enemies, but that however inexcusable the enmity of Ajax had been, his previous nobleness (1355) and bravery ought not to be passed over without the honoured rites of burial. Some MSS. have βροτοῖς, but βροτῶν appears to be the ancient reading, and intrinsically is the best. The genitive is frequently ? used in a similar way with a nominative or accusative adjective, as in O. C. 279, τὸν εὐσεβῆ βροτῶν, but in Od. 17. 589 the case is exactly similar to that of Aj. 1358, οὐ γάρ τού τινες ὧδε καταθνητῶν ἀνθρώπων | ἀνέρες ὑβρίζοντες ἀτάσθαλα μηχανόωνται. Also Od. 23. 187, ἀνδρῶν δ᾽ οὔ κέν τις ζωὸς βροτός. Eur. Iph. Aul. 922, λελογισμένοι γὰρ οἱ τοιοίδ᾽ εἰσὶν βροτῶν. The genitive in these cases is not a mere pleonasm, but is used as a generic term including the whole human race, out of which certain persons expressed by the nominative are said to be distinguished by certain characteristic marks. "Such persons of all mortals are unstable." Such, that is, as act like him are distinguished by this peculiar mark of instability beyond all other men.

ΑΙΑΣ. 109

ΟΔΥΣΣΕΥΣ.
τῷ γάρ με μᾶλλον εἰκὸς ἢ 'μαυτῷ πονεῖν;
ΑΓΑΜΕΜΝΩΝ.
σὸν ἄρα τοὔργον, οὐκ ἐμὸν κεκλήσεται.
ΟΔΥΣΣΕΥΣ.
ὡς ἂν ποιήσῃς, πανταχῇ χρηστός γ' ἔσει.
ΑΓΑΜΕΜΝΩΝ.
ἀλλ' εὖ γε μέντοι τοῦτ' ἐπίστασ', ὡς ἐγὼ   1370
σοὶ μὲν νέμοιμ' ἂν τῆσδε καὶ μείζω χάριν·
οὗτος δὲ κἀκεῖ κἀνθάδ' ὢν ἔμοιγ' ὁμῶς
ἔχθιστος ἔσται. σοὶ δὲ δρᾶν ἔξεσθ' ἃ χρή.

1368, 1369. σὸν ἄρα τοὔργον... χρηστός γ' ἔσει. "Then it shall be called your deed, not mine," that is, the deed of permitting the burial. This is as much as to say, "I give my consent to the burial, provided that you do not make it public, but take it entirely on yourself as your act and deed." Upon this Odysseus replies, "However you act (that is, whether you openly consent to the burial, or only withdraw your opposition to it), in all cases (πανταχῇ) you will be commended as a kindly-disposed man." With respect to ὡς ἄν, cf. Aesch. Eum. 33, μαντεύομαι ὡς ἂν ἡγῆται θεός. τοὔργον could not mean the actual work of burying the dead body. There never was the slightest idea entertained that Agamemnon would take an active part in that work. Throughout the whole dialogue the question of disputation was, whether Agamemnon would consent to the burial, and not a hint was breathed that Agamemnon was expected to take an active part in performing the usual rites of interment. That office would be left entirely to the friends of the deceased.

1373. σοὶ δὲ δρᾶν ἔξεσθ' ἃ χρή. Dindorf has corrected χρή into χρῇς. In his opinion any admission on the part of Agamemnon that Odysseus would be doing what was right in permitting the burial of Ajax, would be altogether inconsistent with his character—"sententia ... plane aliena ab Agamemnonis persona." See note on v. 1350. Throughout the previous dialogue Agamemnon never for one moment disputes the opinion which Odysseus had expressed with so much force and distinctness, that to permit the burial was an act of justice to the man and of reverence towards the gods. Only he was afraid that if he permitted it, he would incur the reproaches of the people. When, however, Odysseus had assured him that such was the strong feeling generally entertained about the justice of the case, that in the opinion of all men (1363) he would be

ΧΟΡΟΣ.

ὅστις σ᾽, Ὀδυσσεῦ, μὴ λέγει γνώμῃ σοφὸν
φῦναι, τοιοῦτον ὄντα, μῶρός ἐστ᾽ ἀνήρ.   1375

ΟΔΥΣΣΕΥΣ.

καὶ νῦν γε Τεύκρῳ τἀπὸ τοῦδ᾽ ἀγγέλλομαι
ὅσον τότ᾽ ἐχθρὸς ἦ, τοσόνδ᾽ εἶναι φίλος.
καὶ τὸν θανόντα τόνδε συνθάπτειν θέλω,
καὶ ξυμπονεῖν καὶ μηδὲν ἐλλείπειν ὅσον
χρὴ τοῖς ἀρίστοις ἀνδράσιν πονεῖν βροτούς.   1380

ΤΕΥΚΡΟΣ.

ἄριστ᾽ Ὀδυσσεῦ, πάντ᾽ ἔχω σ᾽ ἐπαινέσαι
λόγοισι· καί μ᾽ ἔψευσας ἐλπίδος πολύ.
τούτῳ γὰρ ὢν ἔχθιστος Ἀργείων ἀνὴρ
μόνος παρέστης χερσὶν, οὐδ᾽ ἔτλης παρὼν
θανόντι τῷδε ζῶν ἐφυβρίσαι μέγα,   1385
ὡς ὁ στρατηγὸς οὑπιβρόντητος μολὼν,
αὐτός τε χὠ ξύναιμος ἠθελησάτην
λωβητὸν αὐτὸν ἐκβαλεῖν ταφῆς ἄτερ.
τοιγάρ σφ᾽ Ὀλύμπου τοῦδ᾽ ὁ πρεσβεύων πατὴρ
μνήμων τ᾽ Ἐρινὺς καὶ τελεσφόρος Δίκη   1390
κακοὺς κακῶς φθείρειαν, ὥσπερ ἤθελον
τὸν ἄνδρα λώβαις ἐκβαλεῖν ἀναξίως.
σὲ δ᾽, ὦ γεραιοῦ σπέρμα Λαέρτου πατρὸς,
τάφου μὲν ὀκνῶ τοῦδ᾽ ἐπιψαύειν ἐᾶν,
μὴ τῷ θανόντι τοῦτο δυσχερὲς ποιῶ·   1395
τὰ δ᾽ ἄλλα καὶ ξύμπρασσε, κεἴ τινα στρατοῦ

esteemed to be a just man in permitting it, his fears were dispelled, and he says to Odysseus, "I hate the man as much as ever, but you have my permission to do what is right." In saying this, he only expressed what all the previous context goes to show was his moral sense and conscientious conviction about the justice of the case.

1396. κεἴ τινα στρατοῦ θέλεις κομίζειν. "And even if you

ΑΙΑΣ.

θέλεις κομίζειν, οὐδὲν ἄλγος ἕξομεν.
ἐγὼ δὲ τἄλλα πάντα πορσυνῶ· σὺ δὲ
ἀνὴρ καθ' ἡμᾶς ἐσθλὸς ὢν ἐπίστασο.

ΟΔΥΣΣΕΥΣ.

ἀλλ' ἤθελον μέν· εἰ δὲ μή 'στί σοι φίλον 1400
πράσσειν τάδ' ἡμᾶς, εἶμ', ἐπαινέσας τὸ σόν.

ΤΕΥΚΡΟΣ.

ἅλις· ἤδη γὰρ πολὺς ἐκτέταται
χρόνος. ἀλλ' οἱ μὲν κοίλην κάπετον
χερσὶ ταχύνετε, τοὶ δ' ὑψίβατον
τρίποδ' ἀμφίπυρον λουτρῶν ὁσίων 1405
θέσθ' ἐπίκαιρον·
μία δ' ἐκ κλισίας ἀνδρῶν ἴλη
τὸν ὑπασπίδιον κόσμον φερέτω.
παῖ, σὺ δὲ πατρός γ', ὅσον ἰσχύεις,
φιλότητι θιγὼν πλευρὰς σὺν ἐμοὶ 1410
τάσδ' ἐπικούφιζ'· ἔτι γὰρ θερμαὶ
σύριγγες ἄνω φυσῶσι μέλαν
μένος. ἀλλ' ἄγε πᾶς, φίλος ὅστις ἀνὴρ
φησὶ παρεῖναι, σούσθω, βάτω,
τῷδ' ἀνδρὶ πονῶν τῷ πάντ' ἀγαθῷ 1415
κοὐδενί πω λῴονι θνητῶν.
[Αἴαντος, ὅτ' ἦν, τότε φωνῶ.]

ΧΟΡΟΣ.

ἦ πολλὰ βροτοῖς ἔστιν ἰδοῦσιν

wish that any one of the army should take part in the funeral honours, we shall not be grieved;" that is to say, if you will depute any chief who had no personal enmity to the deceased, it will cause no pain either to his friends, or to the spirit of the dead man. His presence will not be unwelcome. Teucer is so highly pleased beyond all expectation with the noble conduct of Odysseus, that he takes care to soften his refusal with this concession. Cf. 1413, ἀλλ' ἄγε πᾶς, φίλος ὅστις ἀνὴρ φησὶ παρεῖναι.

1418—1420. The moral obser-

112 ΣΟΦΟΚΛΕΟΥΣ ΑΙΑΣ.

γνώναι· πρὶν ἰδεῖν δ' οὐδεὶς μάντις
τῶν μελλόντων ὅ τι πράξει.

vation with which the Chorus concludes this drama, although it has a special reference to the unforeseen calamities of Ajax, is of a very wide application. "Much knowledge is imparted to men by the teaching of actual experience, but before he experiences them, no man can foretell the things which will befall him."

"Mortals from what they see
  their knowledge gain,
But ere they see, no prophet's
  piercing mind
The dark events of future
  fate can know."—*Potter*.

APPENDIX.

Line 390.

ἐχθρὸν ἄ|λημα | τούς τε | δισσάρ|χας ὀλέσας | βασιλῆς. The corresponding verse in the strophe is 375, ἐν δ' ἐλί|κεσσι | βουσὶ | καὶ κλυ|τοῖς πεσὼν αἰ|πολίοις, where it may be observed that the trochaic dipodia—τοῖς πεσὼν αἰ—is answered by the choriambus—χας ὀλέσας—in v. 390. This is shown to be a legitimate licence in the following note on 600—609 in this Appendix. All modern editors who have changed ὀλέσας into ὀλέσσας for the sake of a more exact correspondence of the metre than the poet himself ever contemplated, seem to have been perfectly unconscious of the fact, that in the three tragic poets, Aeschylus, Sophocles, and Euripides, the 1st aorist of the verb ὄλλυμι and its compounds is met with more than a hundred times, and yet it is invariably written with only one sigma.

Lines 600—609.

The main objection to the MSS. reading of this passage is the metre, more especially of v. 601. In the corresponding verse in the antistrophe, 614, κρα|τοῦντ' ἐν Ἄρει | νῦν | δ' αὖ φρενὸς οἰ|οβότης, the first choriambus is answered by four long syllables in 601, Ἰ|δαίᾳ μίμνω|, and the second choriambus is answered by a trochaic dipodia, - ‿, - -, λει|μωνίᾳ ποίᾳ|. It must be admitted that four long syllables as an answer to a choriambus is a violation of the laws of metre, but the fault is easily corrected; for if instead of μίμνω we write μένω, we get an iambic dipodia, - -, ‿ -, and I am prepared to show by a large amount of cumulative evidence that an iambic or trochaic dipodia in answer to a choriambus is a legitimate licence. Besides these two, there are six other cases of this licence in Ajax, eight in O. C., one in O. T., and two in Phil. Those in Ajax are the following:—

APPENDIX.

1st. 255. ἔ|πλατος ἴσχει|, answering to
231. |ἐπτωπόμους|.
2nd. 374. ὃς χερσὶ μὲν, answering to
388. προγό|νων προπάτωρ|
3rd. 375. κλυ|τοῖς πεσὼν αἱ|πολίοις
390. δισ|σάρχας ὀλέσας|.
See note on v. 390 in this Appendix.
4th. 616. |ἔργα χερσὶν|, answered by
603. |τρυχόμενος|.
5th. 635. κεύ|θων ἢ νοσῶν|
622. |ἔντροφος ἢ|μέρᾳ.
6th. 1187. |τὰν ἔπαυστον|
1195. |κεῖνος ἀνὴρ|.

Those in O. C. are the following :—

1st. 151. μακραί|ων δ' ὡς ἐπει|κάσαι
120. πάν|των ἀκορέστ|ατος.
2nd. 155. |μὴ προσπέσῃς|
125. ἔγχω|ρος προσέβα|.
3rd. 134. |οὐδὲν ἄζονθ'|
166. |εἴ τιν' ἔχεις|.
4th. 180. ἔ|τι προσβίβα|ζε
195. ἔσ|θω λέχριός|.
5th. 204. αὔδα|σον τίς σ' ἔφυ|σε
185. τλά|μων ὅ τι καὶ|.
6th. 520. ἤ|νεγκον ἄκων|
510. ἤ|δη κακὸν ὦ|.
7th. 516. |σᾶς πέπονθ' ἔργ'|
528. δυσ|ώνυμα λέκτρ'|.
8th. 1050. |σεμναὶ τιθη|νοῦνται
1065. |δεινὸς ὁ προσ|χώρων.

Also O. T. :—

1090. |τὰν αὔριον|
1102. |τις θυγάτηρ|.

Also Phil. :—

1st. 1100. |τοῦ λῴονος|
1121. |καὶ γὰρ ἐμοὶ|.
2nd. 1161. μη|δενὸς κρατύ|νων
1138. αἰσ|χρῶν ἀνατέλλ|ονθ'.

APPENDIX. 115

What is most remarkable in this case is the fact, that wherever the choriambus is answered by four syllables, it is invariably answered by an iambic or trochaic dipodia. There is not, I believe, a single deviation from this rule, except in the case above mentioned, in v. 601, which admits of a most easy correction by changing μίμνω into μένω. It appears that μίμνω is a poetical form for μένω which the Attic poets only used when the metre required the first syllable to be long, but that they had no sort of objection to the ordinary form μένω when the metre required the first syllable to be short; for we find it frequently used in this play, as in vv. 76, 87, 88, 404, and 641. In v. 601 it is most likely that the ordinary form was originally used, and that it afterwards got changed into μίμνω by some transcriber who thought the poetical form preferable; and when once a plausible correction of this sort was introduced, we can easily understand how it would find its way into other copies. In Eur. Med. 440, Ἑλλάδι τᾷ μεγάλᾳ μένει, the metre requires the first syllable of μένει to be short, and yet it is a fact that in one or two MSS. the transcriber has preferred the poetical form μίμνει.

The line of argument which has been here followed out goes upon the extreme improbability of the choriambus being always answered by an iambic or trochaic dipodia, in the case of its being answered by four syllables. If the deviation from a choriambus had happened by mere chance, as it is assumed by the metrical critics, that is to say, through the carelessness of transcribers in writing one word for another, the deviation might have assumed a multitude of other forms in which the quantities of four syllables might have been ranged. Moreover, a like variety of forms would have been seen when the choriambus was represented by three syllables, or by five. This, however, is not the case. First, there are, I believe, only three instances to be met with in Sophocles, where the choriambus is represented by three syllables, and then it is always found that they are three long syllables, that is to say, the two short syllables of the choriambus are contracted into one long one. They are the following:—

Aj. 1187. δο|ρυσσόντων|.
1195. ἔ|δειξεν ὅπλων|.
1190. |εὑρώδη|.
1197. πό|νοι πρόγονοι|.
O. T. 468. φυ|γᾷ πόδα νω|μᾶν.
478. πέ|τρας ὡς ταῦ|ρος.

116   APPENDIX.

Again, whenever the choriambus is answered by five syllables, it is always found that one or other of the two long syllables of a choriambus is represented by the resolution of it into two short ones. The instances of this kind to be found in Sophocles are five.

```
       Aj.  403.  |ὀλέθριον αἰ|κίζει.
            420.  |εὔφρονες Ἀρ|γείοις.
       O. T. 1341. |τὸν ὀλέθριον|.
             1361. |αὐτὸς ἔφυν|.
       O. T. 1195. οὐ|δένα μακαρί|ζω.
             1203. Θή|βαισιν ἀνάσσ|ων.
       Trach. 636. |Μηλίδα παρὰ|.
              643. |ἀντίλυρον|.
       An.  787.  |φύξιμος οὐ|δείς.
            799.  |πάρεδρος ἐν ἀρ|χαῖς.
```

We may here see that in all the above cases the change from a choriambus is restrained within certain very intelligible and definable limits, and that those limits are never transgressed, the change being only allowed in certain well-defined ways, differing according to the different numbers of the syllables by which it is represented. These are facts which, if duly considered, will plainly show that the changes have not arisen from mere accident, that is to say, from the mistakes and blunders of transcribers. To show this more demonstrably, let me observe, first with respect to the change into an iambic or trochaic dipodia, that the combinations of four syllables taken together, with respect to their quantities and the order of those quantities, are, $2^4 = 16$. That I may not be misunderstood as to what I mean, I here put them down, namely—

(1) - ᴗ ᴗ -, (2) - - ᴗ -, (3) - ᴗ - -, (4) - ᴗ - ᴗ, (5) ᴗ - ᴗ -,
(6) - - ᴗ ᴗ, (7) ᴗ ᴗ - -, (8) ᴗ - - ᴗ, (9) ᴗ - - -, (10) - - - ᴗ,
(11) - ᴗ ᴗ ᴗ, (12) ᴗ ᴗ ᴗ -, (13) ᴗ ᴗ - ᴗ, (14) ᴗ - ᴗ ᴗ, (15) ᴗ ᴗ ᴗ ᴗ,
(16) - - - -.

Here it is to be observed that the choriambus itself is one of the combinations. Consequently there are fifteen other ways in which four syllables as to their quantities may deviate from it, and out of these fifteen there are only five ways to be met with in the whole of Sophocles, namely, the second, third, fourth, and fifth of the above list, which may all be included under one law of metre, and the

APPENDIX. 117

sixteenth of the above list, where there is one instance of a deviation, which by a very slight alteration may be rendered conformable to the same law. Is it possible that this could have arisen from mere accident? Then again with respect to three syllables the combinations are $2^3 = 8$, and yet there is only one out of these eight combinations, namely, - - -, which is ever met with in Sophocles as a representative of the choriambus—and it happens to be the only one which appears to be a justifiable deviation from it. But the case of the choriambus being represented by five syllables is the most remarkable. The combinations of five syllables are $2^5 = 32$, and yet out of these thirty-two combinations there are only two which are used in Sophocles, on five different occasions, and moreover, they are the only two which could be justified by the ordinary principles of metre. Viewing this remarkable fact as the result of mere chance, the value of the chance of its happening five times following is, $(\frac{2}{32})^5 = (\frac{1}{16})^5$. Therefore the ratio of the odds against it is $16^5 - 1 : 1$; that is to say, the odds *against* its being a mere accident, and consequently *in favour* of its being the intentional work of the poet himself, is more than a million to one. The same thing may be more abundantly proved of the iambic or trochaic dipodia; for inasmuch as it has been already shown that out of the fifteen ways in which four syllables may deviate from a choriambus, there are only five to be met with in the whole of Sophocles, it follows that the value of the chance is $\frac{5}{15} = \frac{1}{3}$. But it has been already shown, in the previous part of this note, that there are 19 instances of one or other of those five deviations in Sophocles, and not one instance of the other ten deviations. Therefore, assuming, as the metrical critics do, that all these 19 instances are the blundering accidents of emendators and transcribers, the value of such a chance is $(\frac{1}{3})^{19}$. This is such an exceedingly small fraction, that the odds against the probability of their assumption are more than one thousand millions to one. To the above five instances of the resolved form of the choriambus might be added a sixth, namely—

An. 970. Σαλμυ|δησὸς ἴν' ἀγ|χίπολις Ἄρης|.
981. ἆ δὲ | σπέρμα μὲν ἀρ|χαιογόνων|.

In this instance two MSS. have ἀγχίπτολις, which prevents the two lines from corresponding to such a degree, that no writer on Greek Tragic Metre has ever been able to defend it.

APPENDIX.

LINE 905.

τίνος ποτ' ἄρ' ἔπραξε χειρὶ δύσμορος; By Hermann's correction of ἔπραξε into ἔρξε, this verse has been made to agree in metre with its corresponding verse 951, which is a penthemimer (⏑ -, ⏑ -, ⨯), followed by an iambic tripodia. Brunck thought that the fault of metre lay in v. 951, ἄγαν δ' ὑπερβριθὲς ἄχθος ἤνυσαν, and so added τόδ' before ἄχθος. Elmsley was of the same opinion with Brunck. Hermann, on the contrary, not only maintained that the metre of v. 951 was perfectly sound, but that it was in constant use with the tragic poets. "Ibi sanissima est librorum scriptura, quae metrum praebet tragicis usitatissimum." Whatever may have been the practice of other tragic poets in this matter I am not prepared to say, but of this I am well assured, that there are only two instances of this kind of metre in the whole of Sophocles. One of them is O. T. 1204, τανῦν δ' ἀκούειν τίς ἀθλιώτερος ; with its corresponding v. 1211. The other is El. 478, μέτεισιν, ὦ τέκνον, οὐ μακροῦ χρόνου, with its corresponding v. 494. It is further to be observed that each of these two instances is met with in a series of lyric verses, where the metre is frequently changing. This being so, if instead of there being only two instances there had been as many as fifty or a hundred, yet the fact of each and all of them being found in series of lyric verses would not justify the correction of an iambic trimeter into this kind of metre in a part of a poetic work where it was met with under totally different circumstances. Moreover, Hermann says that while Tecmessa speaks in iambics, the Chorus speaks in lyrics. This is only the case when he is uttering a lamentation, but when he asks a plain simple question he speaks in iambics, as may be seen in vv. 892, 894, 895. Hermann did the same kind of thing with O. C. 1677, τί δ' ἔστιν ; οὐκ ἔστιν μὲν εἰκάσαι, φίλοι. He ejected οὐκ, and turned the line into the same kind of metre as that into which he turned Aj. 905, in order that it might agree with the corresponding v. 1704, ἔπραξεν ; ἔπραξεν οἷον ἤθελεν. To say nothing about the utter destruction of the proper sense of the passage occasioned by that correction, he unconsciously introduced a false quantity into the corresponding v. 1704, if he intended, as he certainly did, to make the first five syllables of it a penthemimer; for I believe it will be found to be a fact, that whenever the verb πράσσω begins with ἐ- or with πε-, as in ἔπραξα, πέπραγμαι, &c., the first syllable is on no occasion whatever made long in any one of the *three* tragic poets. With respect to the correctness of the metre of

APPENDIX. 119

O. C. 1677, Prof. Campbell observes that "two iambic trimeters make a natural division between the first and second strophe, just as strophes 2 and 3 are divided by one iambic trimeter." Elmsley's correction of the corresponding v. O. C. 1704, ἔπραξεν; ἐξέπραξεν, is a real improvement in every respect, and is therefore in all probability a restoration of the original text.

LINE 1001.

ἡγεῖτ' οἴκοθεν. It appears to have been a general rule with tragic writers, that "when a trimeter ends with a word of three syllables, preceded by a word of more than one syllable, the syllable preceding the trisyllabic word must be short. The same is the case if the trisyllabic ending, - ᴗ -, is not contained in a single word, but either consists of a monosyllable and an iambus, or a trochee and a monosyllable."—*Linwood, Trag. Met.*

The exceptions to this rule are pretty numerous. Some of these are the following:—

O. C. 1022. οὐδὲν δεῖ πονεῖν.
Eur. Alcest. 682. οὐδεὶς βούλεται.
Her. Fur. 1338. οὐδὲν δεῖ φίλων.
Hec. 729. οὐδὲ ψαύομεν.
Andr. 347. ἀλλὰ ψεύσεται.
Iph. A. 530. κᾆτα ψεύδομαι.

"Such instances as these Hermann accounts for by the stop which occurs after the middle of the verse."—*Linwood.* But no excuse has been invented for such instances as the following:—

O. C. 1543. ὥσπερ σφὼ πατρί.
Phil. 22. σήμαιν' εἴτ' ἔχει.
Ion 1. νώτοις οὐρανόν.
Trach. 640. σωτὴρ νῷν βλάβης.
Iph. T. 1006. γυναικῶν ἀσθενῆ.
O. C. 664. κἄνευ τῆς ἐμῆς.
Iph. T. 580. οὕτω γίγνεται.
Iph. A. 1456. κεῖνον δεῖ δραμεῖν.

Hermann himself retained ἡγεῖτ', and seemed to have been much surprised at the lengthy discussions which the metre of this verse, Aj. 1001, had occasioned. "Metrum hujus versus, supra quam credi potest, miris disputationibus ansam praebuit."—*Herm.* Perhaps he particularly alluded to what may be called a dissertation on the subject in Porson's Preface to the Hecuba. In his Elem. Doctr. Met. 2. 14. 9 he sums up his own opinion on the subject thus: "Sed quis contendat si aliis in rebus aliquando negligentiores fuerunt poetae, numquam eos hac in re aliquid incuriae admisisse?" and he then adds, "Incuriae tribuerim etiam Sophoclis versum in Ajace 1001." Respecting the general rule above mentioned, Porson rightly observes in his Preface to the Hecuba, "Hanc regulam plerumque in senariis observabant Tragici." Yet he endeavours to show that the rule is not only *generally* (*plerumque*) but invariably observed, by suspecting each verse in which the rule is violated of having been corrupted by transcribers. Inasmuch, however, as he has signally failed in his endeavour to prove this, and all his suspicions on that score appear to have had not the shadow of a pretext to bear them out, save his preconceived opinion about the metre itself, we may, I think, safely acquiesce in the judgment of Paley, that "the instances of departure from this rule are sufficiently numerous to show that Porson's so-called canon is only a generally-observed arrangement, resulting from the fine ear for harmony which the Greeks undoubtedly possessed."

LINES 1188, 1190.

1188. τὰν ἄπαυστον αἰὲν ἐμοὶ δορυσσόντων.
1190. ἀνὰ τὰν εὑρεῖαν Τροίαν.

In each of these two lines there is a molossus, – – –; in 1188 -ρυσσόντων, and in 1190 εὑρεῖαν, representing a choriambus in the antistrophe. It is to be observed that there is only one other place in Soph. where a choriambus is represented by three syllables, namely, in O. T. 478, πέ|τρας ὡς ταῦ|ρος, and that in each of these three cases the three syllables are all long. If the emendators had duly considered this fact, they might perhaps have found out that such a thing as that, occurring three times following, was not likely to happen by chance once in five hundred times. Instead of δορυσσόντων, which is the reading of all the MSS. but one, they have taken the reading of that one MS., δορυσσοήτων, because they evidently considered it to be a much fitter correspondent to ἔδειξεν ἔτλων in 1195 than a molossus. But in doing this they must have

APPENDIX. 121

been perfectly unconscious of the fact that, frequently as the word ὅπλον occurs in the three tragic poets, the first syllable of it is always short, unless the final syllable is elided. This proves beyond a doubt that the word δορυσσοήτων in the famous La. MS. is a false reading. With respect to v. 1190, the attempt to get rid of the molossus has been productive of much greater mischief to the text than merely the introduction of a false quantity into the corresponding line. First, they have shortened the beginning of it into ἀν' εὐρώδη instead of ἀνὰ τὰν εὐρώδη. Secondly, they have lengthened the end of it by changing Τροίαν into Τροίαν, without considering whether such a lengthening is admissible: for wherever this word occurs in Soph. or in Aesch., or I believe also in Eur., it is a word of only two syllables. These are comparatively trifling changes, but in consequence of them the words πόνοι πρόγονοι πόνων in the corresponding v. 1199 required to be changed into that most abominable monstrosity, πόνοι πρόπονοι.

LINES 1204, 1205.

τέρψιν ἰαύειν ἐρώτων·
ἐρώτων δ' ἀπέπαυσεν, ὤμοι.

As far as I am able to ascertain the truth of the matter, I have reason to think that this is the way in which the above lines, 1204, 1205, are arranged, in all the best MSS. with respect to the first of them, and in all the MSS. without exception with respect to the second. In three MSS. of inferior note the first ἐρώτων is omitted. According to the old arrangement, the two lines are each of them just of the average length with the rest of the series; but according to their new arrangement the first line is made shorter and the second longer than any other one of the whole series. By the transposition of the particle δ', the first ἐρώτων is taken away from the previous sentence, where it was wanted to explain the meaning of ἐννυχίαν τέρψιν, and it is added to the following sentence, where it is not wanted to explain anything. Perhaps, however, I may find many persons to differ with me in opinion in saying that the bare phrase ἐννυχίαν τέρψιν is somewhat obscure; for it would appear from Wunder's note on it, " ἐννυχίαν τέρψιν ἰαύειν comparari poterit cum Homerico ἀύπνους νύκτας ἰαύειν, ita ut fere sit τερπνὴν νύκτα ἰαύειν," as well as from Plumptre's metrical translation of it, "The pleasure that cometh with sleep," that it means, in their opinion, "a comfortable night's sleep:" and thence it would also appear that the Greek army were deprived of the comfort of a night's sleep during the whole period of the siege of Troy.

LINE 1274.

ἐγκεκλεισμένους or ἐγκεκλειμένους. This verb, wherever it occurs in Aesch. and Soph., is invariably found to be written in the MSS. in its uncontracted form. In Eurip. it is sometimes contracted. Dindorf has corrected it into the contracted form wherever it occurs in these three tragic poets. Even in a fragment of Soph., namely, Ph. Pollux, 7. 193, βλέφαρον κέκλεισταί γ', ὡς καπηλείου θύραι, he has changed κέκλεισταί into κέκληταί without informing his readers of the fact. Lidd. and Sc. go still further. Under the v. ἐγκλείω they say, " Ion. ἐγκληΐω, Att. κλῄω—hence, θύρα ἐγκεκλημένη Plat. Prot. 314 D; ἑρκέων ἐγκεκλημένος Aj. 1274; δόμοις ἐγκεκλημένος Trach. 579; γλῶσσαν ἐγκλῄσας ἔχει Ant. 180 and 505, and Eur. Hec. 1284." Here they refer to four passages in Soph., and to one more in Eurip., as so many proofs of the truth of their statement; whereas it is, I believe, a fact that in all the MSS. which contain the five aforesaid passages, the verb is written out in its ordinary uncontracted form. With respect to the only other reference to an Attic writer, namely, Plat. Prot. 314 D, the writer of this note has not the means at hand of ascertaining whether the testimony of the MSS. be in favour of their statement or against it. All he can say is, that in the edition of Plato which is in his possession it is ἐγκεκλειμένης τῆς θύρας, and not as L. and S. state it to be, ἐγκεκλημένη. Their statement then amounts in effect to a falsification of documentary evidence, because it has the effect of misleading the great majority of those who read it into the notion that the testimony of the MSS. is in their favour. There was, no doubt, not the least intention of falsifying the evidence of MSS. It seems, however, that L. and S. in this matter have been led into an error by mistaking the corrections of Dindorf and others for the genuine readings of the MSS. There is another word about which they seem to have been led into an error by a misstatement of Dindorf, which I take this opportunity of noticing. L. and S. in the sixth and last edition of their most useful Lexicon, under the word εἰς, almost at the outset of their remarks on it, make this observation : " The Trag. and Com. Poets seem to make a rule of using ἐς before consonants and εἰς before vowels, except that the Trag. also admit ἐς before vowels, when a short syllable is required." This observation seems to have been made on the authority of what Dindorf has stated in his note on Soph. Phil. 482, εἰς ἀντλίαν, εἰς πρῷραν, εἰς πρύμνην. In that note, after having rightly informed us that the codex La. and all the best MSS. have εἰς before each of the three nouns, but that others of inferior note have ἐς before each of the three nouns, he goes on to say, "Apparet utrosque ignorasse εἰς ante vocalem dici, ἐς ante consonantem, nisi quod tragici ἐς, ubi metrum postularet, etiam ante vocalem dixerunt." One would naturally infer from this, that in the MSS. containing the plays of Sophocles εἰς was very seldom found to be placed before a consonant, and that in the very few places where it was found, it might be easily traced to the ignorance or the negligence of transcribers. This is by no means the case. Ellendt in his Lex. Soph. has with great labour and industry collected together all the instances where εἰς is used in Soph. before a consonant, as well as all the instances where ἐς is used before a consonant; and from these collections it appears that εἰς is used before a consonant in the iambic senarii, for the most part with the consent of the MSS., about seventy-five times, and with the consent of the MSS. ἐς is used before a consonant in the iambic senarii about seventy times. It appears, however, that in the lyrical parts ἐς before a consonant is much more frequently used than εἰς. "Melicorum ea ratio est, ut regnet ἐς non εἰς."— *Ellendt.* Judging simply from the near equality of the numbers in the iambics, we might be apt to conclude that it was a matter of perfect indifference to the poet whether in the iambics he used εἰς or ἐς before a consonant; but a closer inspection of some of the words before which this preposition is used, would rather lead us to think that εἰς on certain occasions was preferred to ἐς, and on others the contrary. This, however, is a matter of very little moment; but still, truth should be observed in small matters as well as in great, for it is a misstatement by whomsoever it be made that ἐς is always used before consonants and εἰς before vowels in tragic writers, except where the metre requires ἐς. In order to prove the truth of this latter statement, we ought to confine ourselves to those cases where it is a matter of indifference as regards the metre whether εἰς or ἐς were used, and confining ourselves to those cases, it will be found that in Soph., at least, ἐς before a vowel is much more frequently used than εἰς.

LINE 1290.

δύστηνε ποῖ βλέπων ποτ' αὐτὰ καὶ θροεῖς; Dindorf notices two other readings, αὐτὸς and αὐτῷ. These variants seem to have been the attempts of former critics to get rid of a difficulty which they met with in αὐτά. The difficulty is that αὐτὰ has no antecedent, while yet it seems to require one quite as much as its English equivalent, *them*, requires one in an English sentence. It is usually construed as if it were ταῦτα or ἐκεῖνα. Mr. Jebb is the only one, in his note on the passage, who seems to have been aware that αὐτὰ does not admit of being construed as ταῦτα. Accordingly he translates it as if it had ἔπη for its immediate antecedent: "with what face canst thou utter *the words*?" But there is no such antecedent to be met with in the previous context. Moreover, there is some difficulty with the καὶ, which admits of no easy explanation. Mr. Jebb refers to four passages where he considers καὶ to be similarly used. They are the following:—

O. T. 1129, τί χρῆμα δρῶντα; ποῖον ἄνδρα καὶ λέγεις;
Trach. 314, τί δ' οἶδ' ἐγώ; τί δ' ἄν με καὶ κρίνοις;
Aesch. Ag. 269, ποίου χρόνου δὲ καὶ πεπόρθηται πόλις;
Eur. Hipp. 1171, πῶς καὶ διώλετ', εἰπέ.

It is to be observed that in those four passages καὶ refers back either to a previous question, or to some previous information which the interrogator had already obtained upon the same subject as that of the interrogative sentence in which καὶ is found, and that it may be rendered into English by the word *also* or *moreover*.

Thus, O. T. 1129, "What did he do? what sort of a man *also* do you speak of?"

2nd. Trach. 314, "What do I know? but why do you *also* ask me?"

3rd. Aesch. Ag. 269, "But at what time *also* was the city destroyed?" the interrogator having previously heard the fact of its destruction.

So, 4th. Eur. Hipp. 1171, "Having already heard from you that he was destroyed, tell me *how also* the fatal accident occurred."

The καὶ in Aj. 1290 does not appear to admit of any such like explanation. For these reasons I suspect that ποτ' αὐτὰ καὶ in Aj. 1290 are nothing more than the uncertain conjectures of a transcriber to fill up that portion of the line where the writing had been erased, or become by accident illegible. If we compare it with the ending of v. 785, ὁποῖ' ἔπη θροεῖ, it does not seem to be altogether

APPENDIX. 125

improbable that the ending of this line was similar to it, and that the original reading might have been δύστηνε τοῖ βλέπων τοιαῦτ' ἔπη θροεῖς;

QUINTUS SMYRNAEUS.

Since writing these notes of the Appendix my attention has been called to a recent publication on Quintus Smyrnaeus by Mr. Paley, in which he shows that the madness and suicide of Ajax, as described at length in the fifth book of that epic poem, is almost identical with the account of it given us by Sophocles in this play. Among other points of coincidence Mr. Paley mentions the following: "The madness diverted by Athena from the Atridae to the flocks and herds, mentioned in Q. 5. 360; his return to his senses on finding what havoc he has committed, Aj. 305, Q. 5. 456, and his grief in consequence; his suicide by the sword of Hector, Aj. 817, Q. 5. 483; the lamentations of Teucer and Tecmessa, Aj. 895, 992 *sqq.*, Q. 5. 509, 521; the remorse of Ulysses for having been the cause of the suicide, Q. 5. 571; and his expostulation with Agamemnon not to refuse the corpse burial, 1332: all these points of coincidence make it certain that it was not from our Homer that Sophocles drew his inspirations."

Besides these, in reading over the fifth book of Quintus Smyrnaeus I find that there are other points of resemblance which Mr. Paley has omitted to mention.

1st. In Aj. 167—171 Ajax is compared to a vulture, at whose sudden appearance the smaller birds are scared away. So in Q. 5. 297, τοὶ δ' ἀργαλέως φοβέοντο χήνεσιν ἢ γεράνοισιν ἐοικότες, οἷς ἐπορούσῃ | Αἰετὸς ἠίθεν πεδίον καταβοσκομένοισιν, and Q. 5. 435, μηλονόμοι δ' ἀπάνευθε παρὰ Ξάνθοιο ῥεέθροις | πτῶσσον ὑπαὶ μυρίκῃσιν, ἀλευάμενοι βαρὺ πῆμα· | ὡς δ' ὅταν αἰετὸν ὠκὺν ὑποπτώσσουσι λαγωοί, | θάμνοις ἐν λασίοισιν, ὅτ' ἐγγύθεν ὀξὺ κεκληγὼς | πωτᾶτ' ἔνθα καὶ ἔνθα, τανυσσάμενος πτερύγεσσιν· ὡς οἵγ' ἄλλοθεν ἄλλος ὑπέτρεσαν ὄμβριμον ἄνδρα.

2nd. In Soph. Aj. 191 Ajax is represented as fixed to his seat, motionless as a statue, and keeping even his eyes fixed in one direction: so in Q. 5. 328, ἐπὶ χθονὶ δ' ὄμματα πήξας | ἔστη ἀκινήτῳ ἐναλίγκιος, and in Q. 5. 461, ἀλλ' ἔστη σκοπιῇ ἐναλίγκιος.

3rd. In 859 Ajax prays that the Erinyes may avenge his wrongs on the two Atridae, and then proceeds to imprecate vengeance on the whole army. In Q. 5. 467 he does the same, except that Odysseus is mentioned instead of Menclaus.

This remarkable similarity of ideas between the two writers cannot, I think, be accounted for on any other theory than that there were poems relating to the madness and suicide of Ajax extant in the time of Sophocles, which have been handed down to our times, somewhat altered perhaps and rearranged, in that epic poem which goes by the name of Quintus Smyrnaeus.

THE END.

CPSIA information can be obtained at www.ICGtesting.com
Printed in the USA
BVOW04s1039140414

350596BV00014B/592/P